東京大学
THE UNIVERSITY OF TOKYO
教養英語読本 I
ENGLISH FOR ARTS AND SCIENCES: READER I

東京大学教養学部英語部会［編］
DEPARTMENT OF ENGLISH LANGUAGE,
THE UNIVERSITY OF TOKYO, KOMABA

東京大学出版会
UNIVERSITY OF TOKYO PRESS

THE UNIVERSITY OF TOKYO
ENGLISH FOR ARTS AND SCIENCES: READER I

Department of English Language,
The University of Tokyo, Komaba
University of Tokyo Press, 2013
ISBN 978-4-13-082132-2

Contents

Preface

1993年は東京大学の英語教育にとってビッグバンの年であった。

4月の授業開始の日、教養課程に入学してきた3000名の新入生たちが、誕生したばかりの*The Universe of English*——東京大学で独自に編纂された共通教科書——をいっせいに開き、その内容にぴたりと合致したビデオ教材の画面を食い入るように見つめながら、英語の授業を受けはじめたのである。語学の授業でありながら1つの教室の学生が120名以上という大人数で成立させ得たこと、1学期のあいだに2度の統一試験が行われたことなど、名実ともに一つの時代を画する斬新なプロジェクトであったといえよう。

この「英語I」と呼ばれるプロジェクトは、1993年以前の英語教育のありかたへの反省の上に立って企画・実行された。すなわち、それ以前の英語の授業といえば、50–60名ほどの学生のいる各クラスを担当した教師がそれぞれ好きな教科書を選んで、英語のテクストを読ませ、訳させるというものがほとんどであった。教科書としてはシェイクスピアの劇があったかと思えば、メルヴィル、ディケンズなど癖の強い小説家の作品もある。ジョージ・スタイナーの難解な文明評論、そしてバートランド・ラッセルの人生論ならまだしも、ホワイトヘッドの晦渋な哲学テクストまでそろっていた。どこまで深く読ませるのかも教師によってまちまちである。英語学習という観点からは、そもそも深く読ませることに無理のあるものも多々あった。

このような状況を背景に教科書として編まれた*The Universe of English*は、東大生が学ぶべき英語のスタンダードを示したところに大きな意義があった。またそれにも増して、東大生に知的な常識として持ってほしい教養のスタンダードをも示そうとするものであった。その意味で、とんでもなく野心的で先進的な教養英語の教科書だったのである。翌年には2年生用に*The Expanding Universe of English*が出版され、その後1998年と2000年にそれぞれ部分改訂を経て*The Universe of English II*および*The Expanding*

Universe of English II となり、さらに2006年には全面改訂が行われてタイトルも *On Campus*、*Campus Wide* と変わったが、教養英語としての理念の大枠はほぼそのまま受け継がれてきた。

*　　　　　　*　　　　　　*

このたび、折りよくもビッグバンよりちょうど20の春秋を経て、本書『東京大学教養英語読本』(*The University of Tokyo English for Arts and Sciences: Reader*) が伝えられてきた松明を引き継ぐこととなった。名称は「英語I」から「教養英語」へと変わったが、誕生以来「英語I」が高々と掲げてきた理念——すなわち知的な内容をきちんと読んで理解することが、大学で学ぶべき英語の根幹であるという考え方——にまったく変わりはない。いや、変わりがないどころか、語学教育をめぐる議論の中で、「コミュニケーション」という語ばかりがスポットライトを浴びてくるくると舞い踊っている昨今のありさまを見るにつけ、ますます確たるものとなってきたと言わざるをえない。そして、そのことは、今回の編集の作業や注釈をつける際の方針にも大きな影響を与えているのである。

この教科書には、理系・文系のバランスを考えたさまざまな分野やテーマについて書かれた文章が集められている。そして狭い意味での学術論文は避けられ、一般の教養書として市販されている書物が対象とされている。

したがって、英語そのもののレベルとしては、ことさらに難しいものが選ばれているわけではない。文法の基礎があり、そこそこの語彙力のある大学生は、日本語に置き換えることにさして困難を覚えないだろう。しかし、セッションによって差があるものの、ただ日本語に置き換えただけでは「意味」が透明に伝わってこない箇所が多かれ少なかれ存在するはずだ。すなわち、平均的な学習者にとっては、頭の中でそのような第1段階の粗い「直訳」を作成・咀嚼し、文脈にはめ込んで考え、それを別な形で自分流に表現し直して初めて「意味」が分かるというような箇所が、かなり含まれている文章が選ばれているのである。

このような思考プロセスが、英語の使用だけですべて処理されるというのは理想であろう。実際に、本書はそのような能力のある学生が使用することを想定しながら編集されている。しかしそれと同時に、いまだそこまでの英語力を持つに至らない学習者が母語を用いて思考し、授業が行われる可能性をも、本書は排除しない。排除しないどころか、それを前提としていると言わねばならない。ここには、外国語のリーディングが、広い意味での教育の中で、その本質として果たさなければならない役割と密接に結びついた考慮が働いている。

外国語の文章を読む訓練は、古往今来、洋の東西をとわず知的な教育の重要な一角を占めてきた。上に述べたことをもう一度整理すれば、学習者の視点から眺めた外国語のリーディング体験とは、ほぼ次のようなプロセスをたどるべきものと言えよう。

1. あるセンテンスを前にして、単語の意味を調べ、文法をたよりにいちおうの「直訳」を頭の中に描く。
2. この「直訳」をもとの英語と照らし合わせながら、筆者がどんな「意味」を伝えようとしているのかを考える。
3. センテンスの大まかな意味が推測できたところで、それが前後の文脈にどのようにはまるのかを考え、「意味」を修正する。
4. このプロセスを積み重ねて、段落が全体として何を言おうとしているのか、何が段落の要点であるかを理解する。

このようなプロセスを繰り返し練習し、一つの有機的な纏まりとして文章を理解することが、特定の言語の語学力ばかりか、もっと広い意味での言語能力を伸ばすための知的訓練としてきわめて重要であることは言を俟たないだろう。最初に眺めたときには混沌とした無意味な単語の集合体でしかないが、そこに突如として一条の理解の光が射し、文章全体が秩序を持った一つの塊として見えてくる。そんな発見の喜びを学習者に味わわせ、それが独自の力でできるように訓練し、そのことによって知的レベルを引き上げることこそが、英語に限らず、外国語リーディングの精髄であり、存在意義である。

以上のような考えに基づいて、本書のテクストは編集され、注釈がつけられている。

したがって、内容としては、あまりに高度な専門性や特殊な文化的情報を前提とするものは避け、意欲ある学習者が知力を尽くして格闘すれば、そこに与えられている英語表現からその意味へと到達することがおおむね可能であるようなテクストを選ぶことを目標とした。

もう一つ、注釈の「Q」について一言述べておこう。本書を開けば、問題形式になっている注釈の多いことにお気づきになるだろう。それらは、上に述べたようなリーディングの喜びを学習者自身に味わってもらうことを願いながら作成されている。すなわち、単純な単語やフレーズでも、大きな文脈や意味の流れが理解できて初めて語義が決まってくるものについて、「Q」すなわち質問が付されているのである。

*　　　　*　　　　*

将来英語を本格的に使用することになる者にとっては、この教科書を味読し、深く学ぶことはよい出発点になるだろう。試しに、市中の書店に行き、目もあやに並んでいる洋書を眺めてみるがよい。そこで見る教養書に用いられている英語が、本書の英語のレベルと本質的に変わりのないことが分かるだろう。すなわち、英語を日々実用としている教養ある人々は、このような英語を読み、書き、このような内容について話しながら日々を暮らしているのである。本書が読めないようでは、英語のまともな実用などおぼつかない。その意味で、本書はすぐれて実用的な英語の入門書である。

しかし、将来英語を使う可能性の低い者にとっても、本書のような英語の文章で学習することはきわめて大きな意味を持っている。少し背伸びした外国語の文章を読んで、言語能力を鍛えることにより、さまざまなものごとに対処する際の思考を柔軟にし、発想の幅を広げることができる。内容・言語表現ともに、現在の実力よりも難しいテクストに立ち向かおうという意欲をもち、対処するための思考回路を持つことができるようになれば、その分だけ人生が豊かになるであろう。教養とはそのようなものである。何を知っているかではない。考えるすべを知っていることである。そのような能力を涵養することこそが教育の目標にして、理想でなければならない。すなわち、本書は本来の教育に資するための、外国語の教科書たりうることを目指しているのである。

ただに言語技術の枝葉末節のみに拘泥し、このような理想を等閑に付すならば、教育に携わる者として不明にして無責任のそしりをまぬかれない。では、こうしてできあがったものが、はたして理想に近づき得ているであろうか。その成否を断ずることは編者の一人として潔しとしないが、本書はそれを目指したものであることを明言するとともに、今後も目指し続けることをここに誓おう。

この教科書の作成は東京大学教養学部の英語部会のプロジェクトとして行われてきた。数年に及んだ編集の過程で英語部会の主任をはじめ、さまざまの方々のご支援をいただいてきたことに感謝するとともに、最後に、この教科書の編集に特に深く関わってきたスタッフをご紹介しておこう。主として素材収集の段階ではTom Gally、Paul Rossiter、Brendan Wilson、注釈の執筆・整理の段階では河合祥一郎、武田将明、大石和欣、矢田部修一、大堀壽夫、伊藤たかね、菅原克也、そして全体の統括を山本史郎が行った。また、東京大学大学院総合文化研究科博士課程に在学中の柾木貴之、塚田雄一、Pamela Hsiaowen Pengの各氏には原稿の整理を手伝ってもらい、貴重なコメントをいただいた。さらに、東京大学出版会の後藤健介氏と中山佳奈氏には手のかかる本作りの過程を通じてたいへんなご支援を賜った。この場をかりて心より感謝の言葉を述べさせていただきたい。

2013年1月
山本史郎（編者代表）

＊注記
発音記号は［ ］で示し、イギリス式とアメリカ式とで異なる場合は英音｜米音の順に表記した。

Acknowledgements

Grateful acknowledgement is made for permission to reprint excerpts and figures from the following publications.

[Texts]

Sessions 1 & 2

'How to Look at Everything' by David Finn: From *How to Look at Everything*, by David Finn, published by Harry N. Abrams in 2000. Reprinted by permission of ABRAMS.

Sessions 3 & 4

'How the Brain Creates Our Mental World' by Chris Frith: From *Making up the Mind*, by Chris Frith, published by Wiley-Blackwell in 2007. Reprinted by permission.

Sessions 5 & 6

'A Super Tunnel' by Massimo Piattelli-Palmarini: From *Inevitable Illusions* by Massimo Piattelli-Palmarini, published by John Wiley & Sons. Reprinted by permission of John Wiley & Sons.

Sessions 7 & 8

'The Pendulum Clock of Christiaan Huygens' by Lisa Jardine: From *A Point of View*, by Lisa Jardine, published by Preface Publishing in 2008.

Sessions 9 & 10

'The Secret Garden' by John D. Barrow: From *The Artful Universe* by John D. Barrow, published by Penguin Books in 1997. First published by Oxford University Press. By permission of Oxford University Press.

Sessions 11 & 12

'Heroic Contrasts: The Extraordinary versus the Banal' by Philip G. Zimbardo: From *The Lucifer Effect* by Philip G. Zimbardo, published by Random House in 2007. Reprinted by permission of Random House.

Sessions 13 & 14

'Evolved for Cancer?' by Carl Zimmer: From *The Best American Science Writing 2008*, edited by Sylvia Nasar (Series Editor; Josse Cohen), published by HarperCollins Publishers in 2008. First appeared in the *Scientific American*, December 16, 2006. Copyright © by Carl Zimmer. Reprinted by permission.

Sessions 15 & 16

'Easeful Death' by Mary Warnock and Elisabeth Macdonald: From *Easeful Death* by Mary Warnock and Elisabeth Macdonald (pp. vii–xv), published by Oxford University Press in 2008. By permission of Oxford University Press.

Sessions 17 & 18

'Great Inventions' by John Brockman: From *The Greatest Inventions of the Past 2,000 Years* by John Brockman, published by Simon & Schuster in 2000. Reprinted by permission of Simon & Schuster.

Sessions 19 & 20

'Politics, Scandal and Propaganda of Ancient Olympic Games' by Judith Swaddling: From *The Ancient Olympic Games*, by Judith Swaddling, published by British Museum Press, in 1980. Reprinted by permission.

Sessions 21 & 22

'Miss Pinkerton's Apocalypse' by Muriel Spark: From *The Complete Short Stories*, by Muriel Spark, published by Viking Press (The Penguin Group), in 2001. Reprinted by permission.

[Plates]

Sessions 1 & 2

A Man with a Blue Sleeve: Titian, *Portrait of Gerolamo(?) Barbarigo.* © The National Gallery, London.

Rembrandt at 34: Rembrandt, *Self Portrait at the Age of 34.* © The National Gallery, London.

Rembrandt at 63: Rembrandt, *Self Portrait at the Age of 63.* © The National Gallery, London.

Leonardo da Vinci, *Self-Portrait*: Collection of Biblioteca Reale, Torino.

Francisco de Goya, *Self-Portrait*: Collection of Museo de la Real Academia de Bellas Artes de San Fernando, Madrid.

Vincent van Gogh, *Self-Portrait with Felt Hat*: Collection of Van Gogh Museum, Amsterdam.

Albrecht Durer, *Self-Portrait*: © bpk/ Bayerische Staatsgemaldesammlungen/ distributed by AMF.

Ingres at 24 (1804): Ingres, *Ingres (1780–1867) as a Young Man, 1850–60.* © The Metropolitan Museum of Art/ Image source: Art Resource, NY.

Ingres at 79 (1859): *Self-Portrait at the age of 79 years old.* © RMN-Grand Palais (Chateau de Versailles)/ Gerard Blot/ distributed by AMF.

Van Gogh, *A Wheatfield, with Cypresses* (1889): © The National Gallery, London.

Duchamp, *Fountain* (1917): From Wikimedia Commons (GNU Free Documentation License). ［アルフレッド・スティーグリッツ撮影］

Duchamp, *The Bride Stripped Bare by Her Bachelors, Even* (*The Large Glass*): Photograph by Saori Kuroki, collection of Komaba Museum, The University of Tokyo.

Christo, *The Umbrellas*: From Wikimedia Commons (GNU Free Documentation License).

Museo Guggenheim Bilbao: From Wikimedia Commons (GNU Free Documentation License).

Sessions 7 & 8

The Pepys Library: 武田将明撮影。

A polar bear: 斎藤兆史画。

Sessions 9 & 10

A typical African savannah landscape: licensed by www.depositphotos.com/ Gbuglok.

A savannah-like landscape: © Stefan Czapski from [http://www.geograph.org.uk/photo/2966354].

Fallingwater: From Wikimedia Commons (GNU Free Documentation License).

A typical contemporary urban architecture: From Wikimedia Commons (GNU Free Documentation License).

A cave painting of aurochs at Lascaux: From Wikimedia Commons (GNU Free Documentation License), photograph by Prof saxx.

Sessions 11 & 12

Adolf Eichmann at his trial in Jerusalem in 1961 . . . : Getty Images News/ Photographed by Getty Images/ Getty Images.

Sessions 13 & 14

A DNA double helix: © Cornelius20/ Dreamstime.com.

A comparison of the structure . . . : From Tang *et al.*, "The 2.7-Å crystal structure of a 194-kDa homodimeric fragment of the 6-deoxyerythronolide B synthase," 10.1073/pnas.0601924103. © (2006) National Academy of Sciences, U.S.A.

Sessions 15 & 16

The Houses of Parliament (The Palace of Westminster): © Hudyova/ Dreamstime.com.

Sessions 17 & 18

Bales of hay: © Ben Goode/ Dreamstime.com.

Sessions 19 & 20

Lancelotti Discobolus: 斎藤兆史画。

A chariot: © Deskcube/ Dreamstime.com.

Sessions 21 & 22

A set of Spode cup and saucer: 山本史郎撮影。

A set of Royal Worcester cup and saucer: 河合沙和子撮影。

The University of Tokyo
English for Arts and Sciences:
Reader I

1

How to Look at Everything
(Part 1)

David Finn

Donatello, *The Reliquary Bust of San Rossore,*
1424–27. (detail)

The most uncanny experience I ever had looking into the eyes portrayed by an artist occurred when I was photographing "The reliquary of San Rossore," a sculpture by Donatello in a chapel of the church of Santo Stefano dei Cavalieri in Pisa. Fortunately, the sacristan permitted me to spend as much time as I wanted to photograph it from every angle. At one point, when I focused my camera for a close-up of the face, I gasped in astonishment. Looking through my viewfinder at the eyes of the sculpture, I had the feeling that I was looking into the soul of Donatello himself. The eyes of Donatello's sculptures of prophets and other religious figures had always intrigued me, for they seemed to be looking at some spiritual reality that ordinary mortals could

[About the Author]

David Finn: デイヴィッド・フィン。1921年生まれのアメリカの写真家。特に、古代から現代に及ぶ彫刻の写真には定評がある。本章は、*How to Look at Everything*（New York: Abrams, 2000）からの一節。

[3] **reliquary** [rélikwəri|-kweri]**:** 聖骨箱、遺宝箱。ドナテッロは、1425年頃、初期キリスト教殉教者である聖ロッソーレ（San Rossore）の頭蓋骨を収める箱を、この聖人の胸像（ブロンズ）の形で製作した。なお、本文中では "The reliquary of San Rossore" となっているが、ふつう *The Reliquary Bust of San Rossore* と表記される。

[3] **Donatello:** ドナテッロ（本名 Donato di Niccolò di Betto Bardi, *c.* 1386–1466）。初期ルネサンスを代表するイタリアの彫刻家。ページ下の《ダヴィデ像》（フィレンツェ、バルジェロ美術館所蔵）などの作者として知られる。

[4] **the church of Santo Stefano dei Cavalieri:** カヴァァリエーリ広場の聖ステファノ教会

[4] **Pisa:** ピサ。イタリア中西部、トスカナ州の都市。「ピサの斜塔」で有名。

[5] **sacristan:** 聖具保管係

[8] **viewfinder:**（カメラの）ファインダー

[12] Q. **ordinary mortals** とは何か？

Donatello, *David*, *c.* 1440.

not see. But somehow these eyes were different. I could not explain why, but the close-up view of the face mesmerized me, and it proved to be one of my favorite shots when it was subsequently published. Some years later I read an article in a scholarly publication by Anita F. Moskowitz, who suggested for the first time that the sculpture of San Rossore might in fact have been a self-portrait of Donatello, an unexpected corroboration of what I had felt when seeing it with my camera eye.

Subsequently, I had a different but related experience when I studied two self-portraits by Rembrandt in the National Gallery in London. One was painted when Rembrandt was thirty-four years old, in 1640. The stance of the figure is said to have been inspired by Titian's portrait of "A Man with a Blue Sleeve" in the National Gallery in London, which in the seventeenth century was thought to be a portrait of the famous Italian poet, Ludovico Ariosto. The painting had been sold at auction in Amsterdam in 1639, just a year before Rembrandt painted this self-portrait. By taking on the same pose as the Titian portrait, Rembrandt may have been trying to identify himself with Ariosto and thereby stake a claim for himself as a great artist.

The other self-portrait, which is in the same gallery, was painted some twenty-nine years later, in 1669, when Rembrandt was sixty-three years old. This was the year that he died, after having gone through a number of painful trials in the last years

Titian, ***A Man with a Blue Sleeve,*** c. 1510. (detail)

Rembrandt, ***Self-Portrait,*** 1640. (detail)

Rembrandt, ***Self-Portrait at the Age of 63,*** 1669. (detail)

[15] Q. **shots** の意味はどれか？
1. 射撃　2. 試み　3. 写真

[15] Q. **subsequently** の同意語はどれか？
1. later　2. consequently　3. sequentially

[17] Q. **scholarly publication** とは何か？

[17] **Anita F. Moskowitz:** ニューヨーク州立大学ストーニーブルック校教授。イタリアのゴシックおよびルネサンス彫刻の専門家。

[19] Q. **corroboration** の意味はどれか？
1. 裏付け　2. 証拠の確認　3. 論証への協力

[22] **Rembrandt:** レンブラント・ファン・レイン（1606–69）。オランダの画家。肖像画を得意とし、多数の自画像が残されている。

[22] **the National Gallery:**（ロンドンの）国立美術館、ナショナル・ギャラリー。

[24] Q. **The stance** の意味はどれか？
1. 姿勢　2. 態度　3. 立場

[25] Q. **be inspired by** の意味はどれか？
1. ヒントを得る　2. 感激させられる　3. 元気づけられる

[25] **Titian** [tíʃən]: ティツィアーノ・ヴェチェッリオ（*c.* 1488–1576）。イタリア・ヴェネチア派の画家。

[25] **"A Man with a Blue Sleeve":** 1510年頃にティツィアーノが描いた絵画。ナショナル・ギャラリー所蔵。

[28] **Ludovico Ariosto:** ルドヴィーコ・アリオスト（1474–1533）。イタリアの詩人。作品に『狂えるオルランド』（1532）など。

[32] **stake a claim for himself as a great artist** = assert that he should be regarded as a great artist. stake a claim は、本来は「（土地などに対する）権利を主張する」という意味だが、それを比喩的に用いて、例えばhe staked a claim to the deanshipというと、「彼は自分が学部長になるべきだと主張した」という意味になる。なお、『ロングマン現代英英辞典』第5訂版（*LDOCE5*）では、stake (out) a claimが、to say publicly that you think you have a right to have or own somethingと定義されている。本文に照らすと、若く野心に満ちたレンブラントが、自ら偉大な芸術家と見なされようとしてこの絵を描いたという意味合いになる。

[36] Q. **trials** の意味はどれか？
1. 試み　2. 裁判　3. つらい経験

of his life, including personal bankruptcy and the death of his only son. The contrast in the general appearance of the two self-portraits was remarkable. The early painting showed a proud and self-assured artist; the later painting showed a humble, self-denigrating elderly man without pretensions. And when I cupped my hands to focus attention on the eyes alone, I thought I saw something more. Unless it was my imagination, I was convinced that I saw in the eyes of the young man a sense of supreme self-confidence. No artistic challenge would be too daunting for him. He saw himself as a master at the height of his powers. The eyes in the other self-portrait were those of a man who had been humbled by life's experiences. Although only sixty-three years old, he thought of himself as an old man who had suffered painful hardships. His eyes seemed to say that he was long past the feeling of pride in his abilities or of being impressed with his fame. His eyes were weary, almost as if they had seen too much. He no longer looked forward to what life might bring to him in the future. Ironically, in portraying himself in that spirit he produced one of his supreme masterpieces.

Almost as compelling as Rembrandt's self-portraits is the famous self-portrait drawing by Leonardo da Vinci, now in the Royal Library in Turin, which has become something of an icon in the history of art. I wondered if the carefully drawn eyes show a man who feels sure of his analytical ability to reproduce in a precise way what he sees, or what his fertile mind invents. I could not seem to read as much in this drawing as I could in the Rembrandt painting. For one thing, Leonardo showed himself looking away from the viewer, and for another, the eyes did not seem as personal or revealing as Rembrandt's. Still, I thought I could sense the power of Leonardo's brain in those carefully delineated eyes.

Then I looked at many other images in books I have in my library and let my imagination roam. In Goya's self-portraits, did I not see a man who looked at the world with a highly critical eye, a satirical judgment on the follies of mankind, a bitterness about the evils brought about by human cruelty? In

[38] **Q. the general appearance** の意味はどれか？
1. 容貌全体　2. 世間一般への出現　3. 全体的な印象

[40] **Q. self-denigrating** の意味はどれか？
1. 卑下する　2. 自己を傷つける　3. 自信を喪失した

[41] **Q. pretensions** の意味はどれか？
1. 権利　2. 気取り　3. ふりをすること

[42] **Q. cupped my hands** とはどのような動作なのか、自分で試みなさい。

[43] **Q. Unless it was my imagination** = Provided that I was (　　　) just imagining this

[46] **daunting** ⇐ daunt 怖がらせる、怯ませる

[46] **Q. master** の意味はどれか？
1. 主人　2. 支配者　3. 大画家

[51] **Q. long past the feeling of . . . being impressed with his fame** はどういう意味か？

[55] **Q. spirit** の意味はどれか？
1. 気概　2. 気分　3. 精霊

[57] **compelling:** that makes you pay attention to it because it is so interesting and exciting. E.g., Her latest book makes compelling reading.

[58] **Leonardo da Vinci:** レオナルド・ダ・ヴィンチ (1452–1519)。イタリア・ルネサンス期の画家・彫刻家・建築家・科学者。《最後の晩餐》や《モナ・リザ》の絵画は特に有名。

[58] **the Royal Library in Turin:** トリノ王立図書館 (Biblioteca Reale di Torino) のこと。1840 年設立。ダ・ヴィンチのスケッチが収蔵されていることで有名。英語での正式名称は Royal Library of Turin である。

[59] **something of** = in some sense, to some extent

[62] **Q. fertile mind** とは何か？
1. 肥沃な精神　2. 感情豊かな心　3. 創造力あふれる頭脳

[66] **Q. personal** = expressive of the (　　　)

[66] **Q. revealing** = revealing his inner (　　　)

[68] **delineated:** delineate = to describe, draw or explain something in detail

[70] **Q. let my imagination roam** はどういう意味か？ (roam = wander)

[70] **Goya:** フランシスコ・デ・ゴヤ (1746–1828)。スペインの画家・版画家。

Van Gogh's self-portraits, did I not see the eyes of a man who was almost frightened by the beauty he saw in everything around him? I looked at the eyes in self-portraits by Ghiberti, Dürer, Michelangelo, El Greco, Ingres, Cézanne, Matisse, and Beckman. They all seemed to convey something distinctive.

These were, after all, the seers of the world!

By looking at their eyes in their self-portraits, I thought I could not only glimpse something of their inner selves but also have an idea of the special gift that enabled them to see—and portray for us—a unique vision of the world around them.

Leonardo da Vinci, *Self-Portrait*,
c. 1512. (detail)

Francisco de Goya, *Self-Portrait*,
1815. (detail)

Vincent van Gogh,
***Self-Portrait with Felt Hat*,**
1886–87. (detail)

Albrecht Dürer, *Self-Portrait*,
1500. (detail)

[74] **Van Gogh:** ヴァン・ゴッホ（1853–90）。オランダの画家。

[76] **Ghiberti:** ロレンツォ・ギベルティ（1378–1455）。イタリアの彫刻家・金工家・画家。

[77] **Dürer:** アルブレヒト・デューラー（1471–1528）。ドイツの画家・版画家。

[77] **Michelangelo:** ミケランジェロ（1475–1564）。イタリアの彫刻家・画家・建築家・詩人。

[77] **El Greco:** エル・グレコ（1541–1614）。クレタ島生まれのスペインの画家。

[77] **Ingres:** ジャン・オギュスト・ドミニク・アングル（1780–1867）。フランスの画家。

[77] **Cézanne:** ポール・セザンヌ（1839–1906）。フランスの画家。

[77] **Matisse:** アンリ・マチス（1869–1954）。フランスの画家・彫刻家。

[78] **Beckman(n):** マックス・ベックマン（1884–1950）。ドイツの画家。

[78] **Q. distinctive** の意味はどれか？
1. 明瞭な　2. 独自の　3. 差別的な

[82] **have an idea of . . .** = at least partly understand . . .

Jean-Auguste-Dominique Ingres, *Self-Portrait*, 1804. (detail)

Jean-Auguste-Dominique Ingres, *Self-Portrait*, 1859. (detail)

2

How to Look at Everything

(Part 2)

David Finn

Vincent van Gogh, ***A Wheatfield, with Cypresses,*** 1889

Artists open our eyes to the world in different ways. Once we have seen van Gogh's paintings of sunflowers, wheat fields, and cypresses, we may forevermore see those things as he saw them. And the same is true of later artists who have their own way of forcing us to look at commonplace objects in new ways. With Marcel Duchamp's "Fountain," for instance, we look at an ordinary piece of plumbing equipment as a work of sculpture because he took it out of its usual setting in a men's restroom and mounted it on a pedestal as a work of art. The same happens to us when we see Roy Lichtenstein's comic strip paintings. They look almost identical to the real thing, but he has

[6] **Marcel Duchamp:** マルセル・デュシャン（1887–1968）。フランス出身でアメリカで活躍した美術家・画家。その《彼女の独身者たちによって裸にされた花嫁、さえも》（通称《大ガラス》）のレプリカが駒場美術博物館にある。

[7] **plumbing equipment:** 通常は「水洗トイレの設備」。ここでは下の写真にあるとおり、「男性用便器」を指す。

[9] **pedestal** [pédistl]**:** the support of a statue or a vase

[10] **Roy Lichtenstein:** ロイ・リキテンシュタイン（1923–97）。アメリカの画家・ポップアーティスト。漫画の印刷に使われるドット（網点）を描き込み、太い輪郭線や三原色の使用などによって、インパクトのある表現性を追求した。

[10] **comic strip:** 漫画

Marcel Duchamp, *Fountain*, 1917

The Bride Stripped Bare by Her Bachelors, Even (The Large Glass), 1915–23, refabricated in Tokyo in 1980.

seen them in a way that opens our eyes to a new way of looking at these commonplace images—with his clean, sharp lines, with dots and other patterns covering large areas, with bright colors, all carefully composed and painted as if the subject was a vivid landscape. We may make similar discoveries with Christo and Jeanne-Claude's umbrellas, running fences, and wrapped buildings, or Claes Oldenburg's giant shuttlecock, eraser, electric plug, and clothespin. All these are objects that we are so used to seeing that we may not bother to look at them with a sensitive eye until an artist jars our senses and shows us what we have been missing.

Many people make such discoveries in different ways. My wife and I for years have spent Saturday mornings going to what are called in our part of the country "tag sales," sometimes called "estate sales." These are held in private homes near where we live, in New York's Westchester County. Couples may have retired and moved south, or they may have bought a new house, or they may have died. Everything not wanted by the family is up for sale, and this can include hundreds of objects ranging from furniture, to works of art, clothing, jewelry, books, and often an amazing variety of objects that have been collected over the years. When we started our Saturday morning adventures, I felt as if we were invading people's private lives, or scavenging among things we wanted to buy that might have been precious to the previous owners for personal reasons. But my wife has persuaded me that the people who originally owned these objects might well like the idea that others who love the things they owned have now acquired them for their families.

What often amazes me in those tag sales is seeing what people have kept in their homes as mementos, often things of no special monetary value, but which obviously meant something special to the owners. Among the objects I have picked up at these tag sales are an ancient plane that is still sharp, a beautifully shaped scissors, a brass spigot, an African stool, and a miner's gas light. I always feel that I can see something in

[17] **Christo:** クリスト（1935–2020）。ブルガリア生まれのアメリカの美術家。妻のジャンヌ＝クロード（1935–2009）とともに、建築物を包むなどの壮大な「梱包芸術」を展開し、1995 年にはドイツの国会議事堂を「梱包」した。「梱包芸術」の他にも、1976 年にはカリフォルニアで 39.4 km 続く巨大な布の塀（Running Fences）を出現させ、1991 年 10 月には、開くと 8 m 半ある傘を 3100 本、茨城県の全長 19 km とカリフォルニア州の 29 km の地域に亘って立てるというプロジェクトを実行した（下写真）。

[18] **Claes Oldenburg:** クレス・オルデンバーグ（1929–）。スウェーデン生まれのアメリカの彫刻家。日常的な品を巨大化することで知られる。

[19] **clothespin:** 洗濯ばさみ

[25] **"tag sales":** sales of second-hand items（品物に値札 tag をつけるところから）

[26] **"estate sales":** 持ち主の死亡や引っ越しのために家具等を売却すること

[27] **Westchester County:** ウェストチェスター郡。ニューヨーク州の南東部。

[35] **scavenging** ⇐ scavenge = search for（anything usable）among discarded materials

[38] **might well like the idea that . . .** = may probably be happy to think . . .

[42] **mementos:** 思い出の品々

[45] **ancient plane:** 年季の入った鉋（かんな）

[45] **a beautifully shaped scissors:** scissors は複数形だが、単数扱いのこともある。Cf. a pair of scissors.

[46] **spigot:** 蛇口

[47] **a miner's gas light:** 炭化カルシウム（カルシウムカーバイド）と水を反応させ、発生したアセチレンを燃焼させるカーバイドランプのこと（下写真）。昔の坑夫が炭鉱で用いた。

Christo and Jeanne-Claude, *The Umbrellas*, 1984–91.

A miner's gas light

those objects that is especially meaningful, although often I can't explain why.

In the course of my travels, many ordinary objects have caught my eye in the same way, and I have made a habit of making them part of my life. Once when I visited a cotton spinning plant owned by Springs Industries in South Carolina, I was dazzled to see hundreds of spools of cotton thread automatically rotated on holders as the cloth was made. Seeing several spools in a waste-bin, I took one to keep on my office desk. At another time, when I was visiting a steel plant in Johnstown, Pennsylvania, a group of curiously shaped steel objects were stacked on a shelf; the shapes were so striking to me I took one of them to keep as a work of art. In Venice I bought an oarlock for a gondola that looks like a sculpture by Jean Arp. At another time in Lima, Peru, I saw some men on the beach making a large canoe out of reeds, and I couldn't resist picking up one of the reeds that lay on the sand to add to my collection. When I was at a construction site in Bilbao, Spain, where the extraordinary new structure designed by Frank Gehry as the new Guggenheim Museum was being built, I found a wonderfully rusted and partially scarred rectangular section of a metal casing; it now sits on my mantelpiece as a treasured sculpture. In Alaska I found a broken piece of ivory that seemed to be part of a sled; the shape made by the accidental break makes the piece especially striking for me. It now

Guggenheim Museum Bilbao

An oarlock

Jean Arp, ***Cloud Shepherd,*** 1953.

[50] **In the course of** = during

[52] **cotton spinning plant:** 紡績工場

[53] **Springs Industries:** スプリングズ興産。アメリカ屈指の生地・寝装品のメーカー。1887年創業。

[54] **spools:** 糸巻き

[58] **Johnstown:** アメリカ、ペンシルベニア州南西部の工業都市ジョンズタウン。

[60] **Venice:** 水の都ヴェニス、すなわちヴェネチア。運河を行くゴンドラ (gondola) が有名。

[61] **oarlock:** (U字型の) オール受け。右上写真はヴェネチアのゴンドラのオール受け。

[62] **Jean Arp:** ジャン・アルプ (1886–1966)。フランス、ストラスブール出身の画家・彫刻家・詩人。右写真のような彫刻を作ることで知られる。

[65] **Q. construction site** とは何か？
1. 埋立地　2. 建築現場　3. 建物の敷地

[65] **Bilbao:** スペイン北部、ビスケー湾の近くの港市ビルバオ。

[67] **the new Guggenheim Museum:** ビルバオ・グッゲンハイム美術館 (Museo Guggenheim Bilbao) のこと。ビルバオ市にある。1997年に開館した近現代美術専門の美術館。ニューヨークのマンハッタンにあるグッゲンハイム美術館の分館の一つ。カナダ出身のアメリカの建築家フランク・ゲーリー (1929–) の設計。

[69] **section:** 断片

[69] **casing:** 箱や枠など、さまざまな形状のカバーやケース

sits on a tabletop in my dining room. In Ghent, I found a half-dozen small weaving spindles and later tied them together with a string to make an appealing composition. In the Cotswolds, I found an old lock mounted in a wooden frame with a rich patina on the metal casing.

I can't explain my attraction to these objects in traditional esthetic terms—pointing to a beautiful curve here, a striking composition there, a powerful statement about life. They are just objects that appealed to me at a particular moment, and some instinct within me made me want to keep them. The images in my mind were formed by associations of which I was at best only vaguely conscious, and the intersection of these buried experiences with the objects I saw made me want to keep them.

This is the instinct that has led me to become a collector: something in me is touched by an object, and I am prompted to acquire it. There may or may not be a practical value in the object, but I know that just to have it around or in my possession adds something to my life. My wife, Laura, also has this instinct. She collects models of owls, and we have scores of them in our home. She would be hard put to explain why she loves them but her eyes light up when she finds a new one to add to her collection. I collect books, although I cannot explain why. I read as many as I can, but I could not possibly read the thousands of books I have bought over the years. Partly, I know, I buy them because I would like to read them someday; but even if I cannot find the time to do so, having them around me gives me an inexplicable pleasure.

Once when I was in Kenneth Clark's home in Saltwood, England, I asked him about one shelf in his library that contained very large books. He pulled one of them out and was clearly thrilled to show it to me. He probably hadn't looked at that book for years; but he knew that it was there, and occasionally, perhaps, glanced at its spine, along with those of all the other books on that and other shelves and just felt the pleasure of having it in his possession. That is how I feel about the books in my library. When I see them on the shelf, whether I have

[73] **Ghent:** ベルギー北西部の港市ヘント。ゲントとも呼ばれる。

[74] **spindles:** 紡錘（糸を紡ぐ棒状の道具）

[75] **Cotswolds:** コッツウォルズ。イングランド南西部の丘陵。かつて羊毛の交易で栄え、中世以来の伝統的な町並みが点在する。

[76] **mounted** ⇐ mount 張る、はめる Cf. l. 9.

[77] **patina:** 緑青

[78] Q. **traditional esthetic terms** を言い替えている部分を同じ段落から抜き出しなさい。

[79] **esthetic:** アメリカでは aesthetic [iːsθétik | es-] をこのように綴ることがある。

[80] **statement:**（芸術作品で）主題の表現、（表現にこめられた）主張

[81] Q. **at a particular moment** の意味はどれか？

1. ある瞬間に　2. ある特異な瞬間に　3. 人生の特別の機会に

[83] **associations** = mental connections between ideas

[84] **intersection** ⇐ intersect = meet or cross each other

[85] **buried** = vague and obscured, because Finn himself was not clearly conscious of associations that formed the images.

[92] **scores of . . .** = a lot of . . .

[93] **be hard put to . . . :** ～に困る

[101] **Kenneth Clark:** ケネス・クラーク（1903–83）。イギリスの美術史家。

[101] **Saltwood:** ソルトウッド。イングランド南東部の町。

[104] **thrilled** = excited

[106] **spine:**（本の）背

read them or not, they are part of my life, and I feel blessed by their presence.

Perhaps the most fabulous collector I have known of miscellaneous objects is Nathan Ancell, the founder of Ethan Allen stores. Walking into his house in New Rochelle, New York, is an unforgettable experience. There is practically no room to stand in the house, let alone sit down. His tastes are broadly eclectic, ranging from Russian jewel boxes to a bewildering variety of canes, strange objects carved out of wood, models of all kinds, posters, bowls, sculptures, paintings—literally thousands of things. Most of them he has bought at antique shows, and he always has a great time negotiating with sellers to get a bargain price. There was never a plan in his head for what he would do with all these objects; just looking at something that fascinated him and deciding to add it to his collection gave him great joy. One time my wife and I admired a particularly lovely art nouveau sculpture on a shelf (along with dozens of others); Ancell picked it up and gave it to us. We have enjoyed displaying it in our dining room for years.

So how does one look at everything through the mind's eye? The shorthand answer is *with passion*. One can be passionate about anything one sees—*anything* and *everything*. All it takes is the willingness to open your eyes and your heart, and let feelings grow strong within you. What you look at could be a blade of grass, or a branch of a tree, or the shadow on a wall, or a fabulous diamond on display in a jewelry store.

The mind's eye is magical. Through it we can see loved ones who are no longer here, by looking at objects they owned that were precious to them. We can create works of art in our heads out of a special vision that we can nurture within us. One way that we can nurture this vision is by looking at art created by masters. These masterpieces can teach us how to transform what we look at with our naked eye, or what we imagine in our mind's eye. All we need is the will to do so.

[112] **miscellaneous** [mìsəléiniəs]: consisting of many different kinds of things that are not connected and do not easily form a group (*OALD*)

[113] **Ethan Allen:** イーサン・アレン。1932年創業のアメリカの家具メーカー。Nathan Ancell (ネイサン・アンセル、1908–99) は創業者の一人。

[114] **New Rochelle:** ニューロシェル。ニューヨーク州の南東、ニューヨーク市の北東にある都市。

[116] **let alone . . .** = not to mention . . . ; to say nothing of . . .

[116] Q. **broadly eclectic** = (　　　　)-ranging and various

[117] **bewildering** [biwíldəriŋ]: confusing, especially because there are too many choices or things

[120] Q. **antique shows** の意味はどれか？

1. 古代の芝居　　2. 由緒ある展覧会　　3. 骨董品展示即売会

[126] **art nouveau:** アール・ヌーボー。19世紀末から20世紀初頭にかけて流行した美術、デザインの近代的様式。

[130] **shorthand:** 速記の ⇒ 手っ取り早い

[131] **All it takes** = The only thing you need

[135] Q. **fabulous** の意味はどれか？

1. 想像上の　　2. 伝説上の　　3. とてつもなく素晴らしい

[136] **loved ones** は文字どおりには、家族や恋人や親友などを指す言葉だが、婉曲用法で最近亡くなった人 (recently deceased persons) のことも指す。Cf. *The Loved One* (Evelyn Waugh の小説の題名)。

[139] Q. **nurture** の意味はどれか？

1. 育てる　　2. 教育する　　3. しつける

[142] Q. **naked eye** と対照されている語句 (概念) を同じ段落から探しなさい。

3

How the Brain Creates Our Mental World

(Part 1)

Chris Frith

Who's in Control?

Most of the work that scientists do is of little interest outside a very narrow circle of other scientists in the same field. This is as true for physicists as for psychologists. It is said that the great majority of research papers are read by fewer than 10 other people. Many papers are never read at all. But occasionally an observation is made that is so startling that it is discussed widely outside the field of science. One such observation was published in 1983 by Benjamin Libet and his colleagues. The experiment is delightfully simple. All the person in the experiment had to do was lift one finger whenever he or she "felt the urge to do so." At the same time electrical activity in the brain was measured using EEG equipment. It was already well known that there is characteristic change in this activity just before someone spontaneously makes any movement like lifting a finger. This change in activity is very small, but it can be detected by combining measurements from many movements. The change in brain activity can be detected up to a second *before* the finger is actually lifted. The novel aspect of Libet's study was that he asked his volunteers to tell him *when* they "had the urge" to lift their finger. They did this by reporting the "time" that was displayed on a special clock at the moment that they "had the urge." The urge to lift the finger occurred

[About the Author]

Chris Frith: クリス・フリス。1942 年生まれのイギリスの脳神経学者。ロンドン大学ユニヴァーシティ・カレッジ名誉教授。脳の神経画像を用いる手法によって、人間の高度な認知機能を解明しようとしている。本章は、2008 年に Royal Society Science Book Award を受けた *Making up the Mind: How the Brain Creates Our Mental World*（Oxford: Blackwell, 2007）からの一節。

[3] **circle:**（同じ興味や利害で結ばれた）仲間、集団

[5] **Q. research papers** の意味はどれか？
1. 研究論文　2. 研究書　3. 業界新聞

[7] **observation** = a report of something observed

[9] **Benjamin Libet:** ベンジャミン・リベット（1916–2007）。カリフォルニア大学サンフランシスコ校の生理学の教授。人間の意識、とりわけ「自由意志」について先駆的な研究を行った。代表的著作は『マインド・タイム――脳と意識の時間』下條信輔訳（岩波書店、2005）。

[10] **Q. All the person in the experiment had to do was . . .** = What the person in the experiment had to do was（　　　）to . . .

[12] **urge:** 衝動

[13] **EEG equipment:** 脳波計（EEG は electroencephalogram の略）

[14] **this activity** = this electrical activity 電気的活動

[15] **spontaneously** = without a pre-existing intention, without a forethought

[16] **it can be detected by combining measurements from many movements:** 非常に微小な電位の変化は、実験のさまざまな計測値を組み合わせることによって認められたということ。

[18] **up to** = maximum. E.g., The auditorium can seat up to 300 people.

[19] **The novel aspect of Libet's study:** なぜ斬新（novel）か？ 上記の『マインド・タイム』第 4 章に次のようにある――「もし、意識を伴った意志が〔脳活動の電位変化の〕後に続くとすると、私たちの自由意志についての考え方の根底にまで影響を与えるはずです。しかし……意図が意識に現れる時点について、正確な測定をやり遂げることは不可能のように思えました。意識を伴う意志とは、主観的な現象であり、外部からの観察によって直接アクセスすることができません。……被験者にボタンを押させたり……することによって、研究中である手首の屈曲運動にさらに……自発的な行為が加わってしまいます。……1977 年当時、私は再び、この明らかに解決困難な測定の問題に注目しました。被験者は行為を促す意図が意識に現れた経験について『時計が示した時点』を報告できるのではないか、という考えが浮かんだのです。この時計が示す時点は、黙って記憶され、それぞれの試行が終わるごとに報告されることになります。」

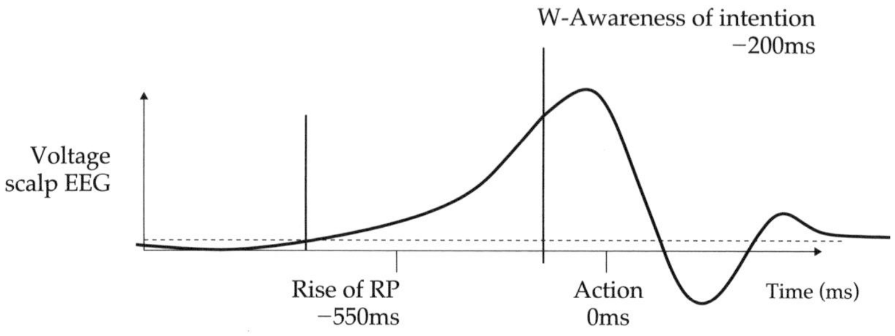

Libet's experiment

about 200 msec before the finger was actually lifted. But the key observation that caused so much fuss was that the change in brain activity occurred about *500 msec* before the finger was lifted. So brain activity indicating that the volunteer was about to lift a finger occurred about 300 msec *before* that volunteer reported having the urge to lift his or her finger.

The implication of this observation is that, by measuring your brain activity, I can know that you're going to have the urge to lift your finger before you know it yourself. This result had such a vast impact outside psychology because it seems to show that even our simplest voluntary actions are predetermined. We think we are making a choice when, in fact, our brain has already made the choice. Our experience of making a choice at that moment is therefore an illusion. And if we are deluded in thinking that we are making choices, then we are also deluded in thinking that we have free will.

But does this result really demonstrate that we have no free will? One problem is that the choices involved are very trivial. It doesn't matter what you choose. In Libet's original experiment you simply had to decide when to lift one finger. In other experiments you might be given more freedom and be asked to choose between the left and the right finger. But these actions are deliberately chosen because they are trivial. With such acts we can look at the process of choosing without interference from social pressures or moral values. The triviality of the action does not alter the fact that when you take part in the experiment you have to decide for yourself precisely when to lift your finger.

[24] **msec** = millisecond（1/1000 秒）

[25] **Q. caused so much fuss** はどういう意味か？

[26] ***500 msec***: 図では −550 msec となっている。RP とは、被験者が行為を実行する前に起こる脳活動の電位変化のことで、準備電位（readiness potential）の頭文字。

[30] **implication:** 論理的帰結。動詞形の imply には「論理的に含意する」という意味があることに注意。したがって、The implication of this observation is . . . は「この発見の論理的帰結として次のことが言える」という意味になる。

[34] **voluntary:** 普通は acting of one's own free will という意味だが、ここは生理学用語として、acting under the conscious control of the brain という意味。

[34] **predetermined** = arranged in advance, decided, fixed, settled beforehand「未来はすべて決まっている（predetermined）」と考え、人間の自由意志（free will）の存在を認めない考え方は、決定論（determinism）と呼ばれる。

[35] **when:** ここでは逆接を意味していることに注意。

[37] **an illusion:** ここでは「幻覚」の意味の不可算名詞ではなく、「思い違い」の意味で可算名詞。

[38] **deluded:** この場合は mistaken の意味。

[40] **demonstrate** = prove; show

[42] **It doesn't matter what you choose:** そのような取るに足らないような行為であるなら、どのようなものを選ぼうが大差ない。

[46] **With such acts we can look at the process of choosing without interference from social pressures or moral values:** 例えば、実験を組み立てるときに、被験者に、妻が夫にぶたれようとしている家庭内暴力の場面を見せて、妻を助けるか助けないかのボタンを押させ、その際に生じた脳波と、被験者がどちらかを選んだと認識した主観的な時間を記録すれば、いちおう同じような実験になり、しかも「自由意志を調べる」という（普通だったら多分に倫理的な含みをもった）表現にふさわしいような実験になるかもしれない。しかしその場合には、明らかに倫理的問題、価値判断が介在して被験者に影響を与え、考慮すべきファクターが多すぎるためにはっきりとした結論は出しにくいだろう。リベットの実験の要点は、単純に肉体的行動と、それに対する自己意識の関係をさぐることだから（しかも、指 1 本でも、肉体を動かすかどうかということは「自由意志」によって左右されるということに変わりはないのだから）、そのような余計な判断や思考や倫理的反応が介入する余地のない形で実験を組んだのだろう。

So Libet's result still stands. At the moment at which we think we are choosing an action, our brain has already made the choice. But this does not mean that the action has not been chosen freely. It simply means that we were not *aware* of making the choice at that earlier time. Our experience of the time at which actions occur does not bear a fixed relationship to what is happening in the physical world.

These unconscious choices are just like Helmholtz's unconscious inferences. We do not perceive the object in front of our eyes until the brain has made unconscious inferences about what that object may be. We are not aware of the action we are about to perform until the brain has made an unconscious choice about what that action should be. But this action is determined by a choice that we have previously made freely and deliberately. We have agreed to cooperate with the experiment. We may not know precisely which action we are going to perform at any one moment. But we have already selected the small set of actions from which this precise action will be chosen.

My Brain Can Act Perfectly Well without Me

In Libet's experiment we seem to lag behind what our brain is doing. But we do catch up in the end. In other experiments our brain controls our actions and we don't even know about it. This is the case in the "double-step" experiment in which your task is to look out for a target that is a vertical rod. As soon as it appears you reach for it with your hand and grasp it. Reaching and grasping is something you can do very easily and rapidly. Here, the trick is that on some occasions, as soon as you start to move your hand, I move the target to a new position. You can easily adjust to this and will accurately grasp the target in its new position. On many of these occasions you will not notice that the target moved. But your brain notices the movement.

Your hand starts moving toward the first position of the target and then, about 150 msec after the target position changes, your hand movement changes in order to reach the target in its

[56] **Q. bear a fixed relationship to** はどういう意味か？

[57] **what is happening in the physical world:** 脳内の神経細胞活動など。

[58] **Helmholtz's unconscious inferences:** ドイツの物理学者・生理学者であったヘルマン・フォン・ヘルムホルツ（1821–94）はエネルギー保存の法則を確立したことで有名だが、眼の知覚作用についても大きな功績を残した。ヘルムホルツは眼が物理的にはかなり粗雑な機械であり、それによって捉えうる像と、人間の視覚的知覚のあいだには大きな開きがあることに気づいた。そしてこのことから、人間の知覚はなんらかの「無意識的な推論」の結果として成立しているものだと考えた。

ヘルムホルツの「無意識的な推論」の例：螺旋に見えるが、実は同心円の集まりでしかない。同心円だという事実を確認した後でも、螺旋に見えてしまうのは、眼から入ってきた情報を脳が「修正」してしまうから。

[59] **Q. We** と **the brain** はどう違うのか？

[65] **We have agreed to cooperate with the experiment:**「自分で決断する前に脳が決定している以上、人に自由意志はない」とする意見に対して、そもそも「指を上げるという行為そのものをしよう（＝実験に参加しよう）」と決断したのは自由意志だと言わんとしている。

[70] **lag behind . . . :** ～より遅れている

[74] **Q. look out for . . .** はどういう意味か？

[75] **Q. reach for it** の意味はどれか？

1. それに届く　2. それをつかむ　3. それに向かって手を伸ばす

new position. So your brain notices that the target has moved and your brain alters the movement your hand is making so that you can reach the new target position. And all this can happen without you noticing anything. You don't notice either the change in position of the target or the change in your hand movement. You will tell me that the target only moved once.

In this case your brain can produce appropriate actions when you don't even know that such actions are needed. In other cases your brain can produce appropriate actions even though these are different from the actions you think should be made.

In this experiment you are sitting in the dark. I show you (briefly) a target dot inside a frame. Immediately afterwards I show you (briefly) the target inside the frame again. This time the target is still in the same place, but the frame has moved to the right. If I ask you to describe what happened, you will say, "the target moved to the left." This is a typical visual illusion in which your visual brain has wrongly decided that the frame stayed still and so the target must have moved. But if I ask you to *touch* where you think the target was, then you will touch the correct point on the screen — your pointing is unaffected by any movements of the frame. So your hand "knows" that the target has not moved even though you think that it has.

These observations show that your body can interact with the world perfectly well even though you don't know what your body is doing and also when what you think you know about the world is wrong. Your brain may be directly connected to your body, but the knowledge that your brain gives you about the state of your body seems to be as indirect as the knowledge it gives you about the outside world. Your brain doesn't tell you when your body moves in a different way from what you intended. Your brain can trick you into thinking that your body is in a different place from where it really is. And these are all examples of a normal brain interacting with a normal body. When things go wrong the brain becomes really creative.

[96] **In this experiment:** 今度の（次の）実験では

[101] **visual illusion** = optical illusion

[102] **visual brain:** 脳の視覚野

[111] **Q. what you think you know about the world is wrong** とは、今述べられた実験の場合は、何を指すか？

[117] **Q. trick you into thinking . . .** はどういう意味か？
Cf. be deluded in thinking (l. 37).

同じ円の大きさが異なって見えるのは、脳が、あなたが知らないうちに、右のほうが大きいと判断しているからである。

下の A と B は、どちらが濃く見えるだろうか？
巻末の切り抜き窓をあてはめて A と B の濃さは同じであるという事実を認識したうえで、切り抜き窓を外して脳が補正を加えた知覚との discrepancy を体感しよう。

4

How the Brain Creates Our Mental World

(Part 2)

Chris Frith

There's Nothing Wrong with Me

People with damage toward the back of the brain, usually on the right, often have a left arm which is paralyzed and insensitive to touch. But such people seem to be unaware of the paralysis and deny that there is anything wrong with them (anosognosia). V. S. Ramachandran has interviewed many of these people. His reports illustrate the remarkable discrepancy between what these people believe and their actual abilities.

The left side of Mrs. F. D.'s body is completely paralyzed as the result of a stroke.

V.S.R.: Mrs. F. D., can you walk?
F.D.: Yes.
V.S.R.: Can you move your hands?
F.D.: Yes.
V.S.R.: Are both hands equally strong?
F.D.: Yes, of course they are.

Some people, however, seem to recognize that they are not using one arm and have to explain why.

V.S.R.: Mrs. L. R., why aren't you using your left arm?
L.R.: Doctor, these medical students have been prodding

[6] **anosognosia:** 病態失認、病識欠損症

[6] **V. S. Ramachandran:** ヴィラヤヌル・S・ラマチャンドラン (1951–)。インド生まれのアメリカの心理学・神経病理学者。カリフォルニア大学サンディエゴ校の教授。家族・恋人などが別人に入れ替わっていると錯覚してしまうカプグラ症候群や、幻肢痛など種々の精神疾患を扱い、意識の問題に迫った『脳のなかの幽霊』山下篤子訳 (角川書店、1999) の共著者として知られる。

[20] Q. **prodding** とはどういう意味か？

オリヴァー・サックス著 *The Man Who Mistook His Wife for a Hat* (1985; 高見幸郎・金沢泰子訳『妻を帽子とまちがえた男』早川書房、2009) は、マイケル・ナイマンが同題のオペラ (1986) にし、ピーター・ブルックが劇 *The Man Who* (1995) にした。

表題に掲げられているのは、普段はごく普通の人なのだが、ドアノブに話しかけたり、妻を帽子とまちがえたりする視失認に陥った男性についての話。ほかに、左という概念がなく、自分の右側しか認識できない女性のケースや、トゥレット症候群という、衝動的に体を動かしたり奇声をあげたりする患者のケースなども取り上げられている。

24 歳の男性レイは、4 歳のときからチックが止まらず、奇声や汚言を発するために何度も仕事をクビになっていた。医者のサックスは、投薬によってその症状をおさえると、彼のジャズドラマーとしての即興性や機敏さが失われることを発見する。

「障碍は治さなければいけない、社会生活に適応できなければいけない」という思い込みは誤りであることを教えてくれる本である。

me all day and I'm sick of it. I don't want to use my left arm.

Most remarkable of all are the people who believe they have moved their paralyzed arm when no such movement has taken place.

V.S.R.: Can you clap?
F.D.: Of course I can clap.
V.S.R.: Will you clap for me?
She proceeded to make clapping movements with her right hand as if clapping with an imaginary hand near the midline.
V.S.R.: Are you clapping?
F.D.: Yes, I am clapping.

Mrs. F. D.'s brain seems to have created the experience of moving her left arm when no such movement actually occurred.

In these people it is not simply their knowledge about the positions of parts of their body that is wrong. Their knowledge about whether or not they are acting on the world is also wrong. They believe they are acting on the world when, in fact, they are doing nothing. But imagine how alarming it would be if you were sitting quietly doing nothing and one of your hands started acting all by itself. This can sometimes happen in people with brain damage. The willful hand is described as "anarchic." The anarchic hand grasps door knobs or picks up a pencil and starts to scribble with it. People with this syndrome are upset by the actions of the hand: "It will not do what I want it to do." They will often try to prevent it from moving by grasping it firmly with the other hand. In one case the person's left hand would tenaciously grasp any nearby object, pull at her clothes, and even grasp her throat during sleep. She slept with the arm tied to the bed to prevent such nocturnal misbehavior.

Daniel Wegner has proposed that we have no direct knowledge of causing our actions. All we *know* is that we have the intention to act, and then, a little later, the action occurs. We *infer* that our intention caused the action. But Wegner didn't just stop with this speculation. He did some experiments to test the

[30] ***midline*:**【動物】正中線。動物体を左右に等分する縦の線。

[37] **Q. acting on the world** はどういう意味か？

[41] **Q. all by itself** はどういう意味か？

[42] **Q. willful** の意味に近いのはどれか？
1. 故意の　2. 強情な　3. 勝手気ままな

[42] **anarchic:**「無政府主義の」という意味もあるが、ここは「勝手な」。

[48] **Q. would** の意味はどれか？
1. 〜だろう（推測）
2. よく〜したものだ（繰り返された動作）
3. どうしても〜しようとする（強い意志）

[48] **tenaciously [tənéiʃəsli]:** しつこく（しっかりつかんで離さない様子）

[48] **Q. pull at** はどういう動作か？

[51] **Daniel Wegner:** ダニエル・ウェグナー（1948–）。カナダ生まれのアメリカの社会心理学者。ハーヴァード大学教授。著作 *The Illusion of Conscious Will*（2002）などで、自由意志があると思っているのは幻想だと論じる。

[51] **proposed:**（仮説として）提唱した

[51] **Q. we have no direct knowledge of causing our actions** = we cannot (　　) know that we are causing our own actions

スタンリー・キューブリックの映画『博士の異常な愛情または私は如何にして心配するのを止めて水爆を愛するようになったか』（1964）——『2001年宇宙の旅』（1968）、『時計じかけのオレンジ』（1971）とともにSF 3部作と呼ばれる——のなかで、ピーター・セラーズ演じるストレンジラヴ博士の右手は、勝手に動き出してナチス式敬礼をしたりする。ついには博士自身が、右手に襲われ、左手でそれを阻止しようとする。この右手は、人間のなかに潜在化している暴力性、衝動を象徴するものであるが、実際に自分の手がコントロールできなくなる「他人の手症候群」という症例がある。詳しくは、トッド・E・ファインバーグ『自我が揺らぐとき——脳はいかにして自己を創りだすのか』吉田利子訳（岩波書店、2002）を参照のこと。

idea. He predicted that, if an action occurred after you had the intention to act, then you would assume that you had caused the act even when it was actually caused by someone else. The experiment is quite tricky in all senses of the term. When you take part in this experiment you have a companion (who is really a stooge of the experimenter). You and your companion place your right forefingers on a special mouse. By moving this mouse around you move a pointer on a computer monitor. There are lots of objects on the screen. Through earphones you hear someone name one of the objects. You think about moving the pointer toward the object. If your companion moves the pointer toward the object at that moment (he is also instructed through earphones), then you are very likely to think that you made the movement. Of course the timing is critical. If the mouse moves just before you had the thought, then you don't feel you caused it. If the mouse moves too long afterwards, then you don't feel you caused it either. If the interval is about 1 and 5 seconds between having the thought and the mouse moving, then you will believe you have moved your arm even when this is not actually the case.

Where Is the "You"?

My aim in this essay is to convince you that you do not have privileged access to knowledge about your own body. To do this I have presented my observations from various stages in the hierarchy of knowledge through which you make your body act on the world. At the bottom level there is knowledge about the position of your body in space. This knowledge is crucial when reaching for things. You are very good at reaching. Yet you know very little about the exact position of the various parts of your body in space, and what you know can sometimes be wrong. At the next level there is knowledge about when and how to move, also crucial for reaching. You are good at making rapid reaching movements and can correct them in mid-flight. Yet you may not even know that you have made these rapid and accurate corrections. At the next level there is knowledge

[56] **predicted:** 予言した。Cf. pre-(前もって)+ dict (言う), cf. dictionary.

[59] Q. **the term** とはどの語のことか？

[61] Q. **stooge** [stúːdʒ] の意味はどれか？

1. スポンサー　2. オブザーバー　3. アシスタント

[68] Q. **you are very likely to think . . .** = the probability is very (　　) that you think . . .

[69] Q. **critical** の意味はどれか？

1. 危険な　2. 批判的な　3. きわめて重要な

[75] Q. **this is not actually the case** = you did (　　) move your arm

[88] Q. **mid-flight** の意味はどれか？

1. 空を飛んでいるときに　2. 逃げる途中で　3. 動作の真っ最中に

デカルトが「我思う、故に我あり」と言って以来、哲学者は「我」つまり「自己」の存在を前提にして議論を進めてきた。しかし、「自己」とは何か。そもそもどうやって自己認識ができているのだろう？ 実は自己認識など誰もできていないのではないか？

精神分析家のカレン・ホーナイは、「自己」とは、今ある自分の心身の総体としての現実的自己、潜在的な可能性を持つ実在的自己、さらに理想化された自己という3つに分類できるという。

今ある自分に満足せず、望むべき自分、こうなりたいと願う自分になれと、よくいう。(Cf.「こうありたいと願う自分になるのが怖いのね」、シェイクスピア『マクベス』。)

この教科書を読む前のあなたと、読んだあとのあなたはもはや同じではない。自己は刻一刻と変化している。とすれば、そんなとりとめもない自己をどうやって認識できるのか？

that you are the actor who is making the movements. Even on this fundamental point you may sometimes be wrong. How will this exercise end? Is there anything that you know about yourself? What is there left of "you" if you are not aware of your body or your actions? [95]

[93] **Q. exercise** は、この文脈では何を意味しているのか？

認知科学、脳科学、身体心理学などに興味のある人は、以下の本を読んでみよう。

○下條信輔『「意識」とは何だろうか――脳の来歴、知覚の錯誤』講談社現代新書（講談社、1999）
○下條信輔『サブリミナル・マインド――潜在的人間観のゆくえ』中公新書（中央公論社、1996）
○下條信輔『サブリミナル・インパクト――情動と潜在認知の現代』ちくま新書（筑摩書房、2008）
○春木豊『動きが心をつくる――身体心理学への招待』講談社現代新書（講談社、2011）
○安西祐一郎『心と脳――認知科学入門』岩波新書（岩波書店、2011）
○坂井克之『心の脳科学――「わたし」は脳から生まれる』中公新書（中央公論新社、2008）
○トール・ノーレットランダーシュ『ユーザーイリュージョン――意識という幻想』柴田裕之訳（紀伊國屋書店、2002）
○前野隆司『脳はなぜ「心」を作ったのか――「私」の謎を解く受動意識仮説』ちくま文庫（筑摩書房、2010）

5

A Super Tunnel

(Part 1)

Massimo Piattelli-Palmarini

A mental tunnel is a kind of cognitive illusion. When we try to solve a problem or make a decision, we usually imagine that we are using reason to do this. Cognitive science, however, has shown that in many cases, rather than using reason, we use a form of intuition and adopt—usually unknowingly—a number of rules which are not just different from but also incompatible with reason. A mental tunnel is thus a kind of spontaneous shortcut in our thinking which leads us to a solution which we are convinced is correct and rational; we are so convinced, in fact, that even when our solution can be shown to be both incorrect and irrational, we still continue to insist on the rightness of our answer. Even the finest and best-trained minds can get trapped in such mental tunnels.

One of the best-known examples of a mental tunnel is known as the Monty Hall problem (or paradox) after the presenter of the well-known television show *Let's Make a Deal.*

The Three-Box Game, or the Monty Hall Paradox

Though there are a number of different variations, I offer here the one I find most easy to visualize.

> On a table are three identical boxes, each with a lid, and also a neat pile of ten-dollar bills. This game is to be

[About the Author]

Massimo Piattelli-Palmarini: マッシモ・ピアテリ＝パルマリーニ（1942–）。アリゾナ大学教授。専門は認知科学。本章は、*Inevitable Illusions: How Mistakes of Reason Rule Our Minds*（Hoboken, NJ: Wiley, 1996）からの一節。

[Title] **tunnel** [tʌ́nl]

[1] **cognitive** = connected with the mental processes of understanding

[3] Q. **reason** と対立する概念は何か？ 同じ段落から選びなさい。

[5] **unknowingly** = without knowing it; unconsciously; unwittingly

[6] **incompatible** [ìnkəmpǽtəbl] = inconsistent; discordant; conflicting; incongruous

[7] Q. **spontaneous** の意味はどちらか？

1. 知らず知らずやっている（acting unknowingly）
2. 強制されたわけでなく自発的な（arising from internal forces）

[12] **minds:**（特に、優れた）頭脳の持ち主

[13] Q. **such mental tunnels** とは、どういうことか？ ⇒ある解決に至るまでの思考の過程をトンネルに譬えているわけだが、その過程で人は（　　　）を用いて判断しているつもりでいて、実はある種の（　　　）で判断しているという、そういった思考過程のこと。（tunnels が複数形なのは、さまざまな思考がありうるから。）

[15] **Monty Hall:** モンティ・ホール（1921–2017）。カナダ生まれの演出家、俳優、TV パーソナリティ。*Let's Make a Deal* の司会者として知られる。右の写真の人物。

Monty Hall

[15] **the Monty Hall problem:** モンティ・ホール問題（Monty Hall paradox とも）。確率論の有名な問題。

[15] **after . . . :** ～にちなんで名づけられた

[16] ***Let's Make a Deal***: 1963 年から現在まで続いているアメリカのテレビのクイズ番組

[19] **visualize:** 心に思い描く

[21] **a neat pile of . . . :** 整然と積み上げられた～

[21] Q. **This game is to be repeated** とはどういう意味か？

> repeated a great many times.
>
> Here are the rules for each game, and every game proceeds in identical fashion. First, you leave the room, and while you are out, I put a ten-dollar bill in one of the three boxes. I then close the boxes. I know in which box the money is, but you don't. Now I invite you back into the room and you try to guess which box contains the ten-dollar bill. If you guess correctly, you win ten dollars.
>
> Each game is divided into two distinct phases. In the first, by doing no more than pointing (you are not to touch, weigh, or in any way inspect or manipulate any of the three boxes), you indicate your irrevocable choice among the three boxes, which remain closed.
>
> As you have made your choice, I open another box, one of the two remaining boxes. That box will always be an empty box—remember that I know in which box the ten-dollar bill is. (This means that if you have, without knowing it, chosen an empty box, I will open the other empty box. If, on the other hand, you have unknowingly chosen the right box, I will open either one of the other two boxes.) Having seen one empty box (the one just opened) you now face two closed boxes, one of which must contain the ten-dollar bill.
>
> Now comes the second phase. I now offer you the chance to stay with your first choice, or to switch your choice to the other closed box, the one you failed to choose the first time around.
>
> This will be repeated countless times, and each time, if your second choice is right, you win ten dollars. You leave the room and the game starts all over again.

Now here's the problem: As a general rule, are you better off sticking to your first choice, or switching? What is the best strategy? Think carefully, and ask your friends. Don't tell them right away that the very best minds have fallen into this trap, many of them still believing they were right when they were proven wrong!

[30] **two distinct phases:** はっきりと分かれた 2 段階

[31] Q. **you are not to touch** = you (　　　) not touch

[32] **manipulate** = handle; touch; finger

[33] Q. '**your irrevocable** [irévəkəbl] **choice**' means that you cannot (　　　) your mind once you've made a (　　　).

[34] Q. **which remain closed** = without (　　　) any of the boxes

[47] **the first time around:** 第 1 回目に

[52] **better off . . . ing:** ～すればもっとよい。100 行目も参照のこと。
Cf. better off (⇐ well off 裕福な、満足な).

[53] Q. **sticking to your first choice** と同じ意味の表現をここに引用されたゲームの説明部分から指摘しなさい。

[54] **strategy:** (大方針としての) 戦術、戦略。E.g. His strategy was to hold the Hudson River and isolate the New England States.
Cf. tactics (個別の場面での) 戦術、戦法、駆け引き。

[55] **the very best minds:** 注 [12] 参照のこと。

[56] **they were proven wrong** = it was proved that they were wrong

I have come up against all sorts of responses. Some have insisted passionately that you should *always* switch choices; others have argued that you should *always* stick to your first choice; and still others hold that it doesn't matter at all, that you should now switch, now stick to your first choice. There are also those who, believe it or not—because they think it makes no difference—think they should always switch, or always stick with their first choice. When asked why, they will respond, "Because that's the way it is!" or "I'm basically conservative" or "I like change."

To put a little order into this kind of mental confusion, let me stipulate right away that if there were really no difference at all between sticking to your first choice or switching, if the probability of choosing the box containing the ten-dollar bill were really 50/50, then there would be no motive whatsoever for switching your choice, for sticking to it, or for adopting any other strategy you might devise, such as tossing a coin. But is the probability really 50/50? Your intuition tells you that you face two boxes, and one of them must contain the ten-dollar bill, though you don't know which. Therefore the probability *must* be 50/50. Wrong! The box you chose first has, and always will have, a one-third chance of being the right one. The other two, combined, have a two-thirds chance of containing the ten-dollar bill. But at the moment when I open the empty box, then the other one, *alone*, will have a two-thirds probability.

Hence you should *always* switch. Switching increases the probability from one-third to two-thirds. This runs totally contrary to our intuition, but is rationally absolutely right. The sum of the probabilities of the two closed boxes is, indeed, 1, but the two probabilities are *not* equal. The big point is that the two possibilities do not *need* to be equal. In fact, owing to the way in which this game is constructed, they are *un*equal.

Given that a lot of first-rate minds angrily reject this conclusion, let's justify our switching in another way. Suppose, for instance, that your original choice was the right one; then when I open my empty box, for you to switch will *certainly* (not just probably) penalize you. If, on the other hand, your first choice

[58] **come up against** = encounter（face, come across）, especially a problem

[61] **that you should now switch, now stick to your first choice:** この部分も hold の目的語。

[63] **Q. believe it or not** の意味はどれか？
1. さもありなんと思うだろうが
2. 信じる人も信じない人もいるが
3. 信じがたいと思うかもしれないが

[66] **Q. that's the way it is** の意味はどれか？
1. それが私の道なのさ　2. これぞ突破口だ　3. そういうものなのさ

[68] **Q. order** の意味はどれか？　1. 秩序　2. 注文　3. 命令

[69] **stipulate:** 明言する、はっきりと述べる

[71] **were:** 仮定法に注意。つまり、本当は fifty-fifty ではない。

[74] **devise** = think out, invent

[82] **the other one, *alone*, will have a two-thirds probability:** 最初に選ばなかった 2 つに当たりがある確率は 3 分の 2 であり、その 2 つのうち、ハズレの箱をとりのぞいて残った 1 つの箱は、1 つになっても（*alone*）当たる確率は 3 分の 2 という理屈。

[84] **runs totally contrary to our intuition** = is totally counterintuitive

[85] **rationally:** 理屈として

[86] **Q. the two probabilities** とは何か？

[90] **Given** = In the light of the fact that . . .（Since it is known that . . .）

[93] **for you to switch:** これが動詞 penalize の主語である。

[94] **penalize** [píːnəlàiz] **you:** あなたを罰する（あなたに損害をあたえる）⇒ ハズレとなる

[94] **your first choice was of an empty box** = your first choice was that [=the choice] of an empty box

場合分けして話を整理すると、以下のようになる。

第 2 段階で変更しない場合

第 1 段階と同じく、正解を選ぶ確率は 3 分の 1。

第 2 段階で変更する場合

第 1 段階で正解を選んでいた場合は、必ずハズレを選ぶことになる。この確率は 3 分の 1。

第 1 段階でハズレを選んでいた場合は、必ず正解を選ぶことになる。この確率は 3 分の 2。

したがって第 2 段階で変更する場合に正解を選ぶ確率は 3 分の 2 となり、変更しない場合の 2 倍の確率となる。

was of an empty box, you will *certainly* (not just probably) gain by switching. We have gained a little security. Let's now use that. How often do you think your choice will be correct (and thus *necessarily* penalized if you switch)? One in three times. And how often will you choose an empty box (and thus be *necessarily* better off switching)? Two times out of three.

That is why the best strategy is always to switch. You're going to win two out of three times. Yet I know from long experience that although this explanation is rationally convincing, many people still resist it—which goes to show that even with a clear argument, our initial intuition is hard to overcome. There are some highly intelligent people who simply do not accept this explanation. After a few seconds of hostile silence, they insist on starting all over again from the beginning. They want to go back to the point at which the other two boxes are still closed and they do not know which box contains the money. They refuse to accept everything that happened *before* that point, and everything that may happen *afterward*; they are firmly anchored in their primary, irresistible intuition, which tells them that, if there are two boxes on the table, the probability must be 50/50 that one of them contains the money.

Another momentous decision to make

[96] **a little security:**（議論のための）ある程度しっかりした土台、もしくはある程度の確信（certainty）

[108] **Q. they insist on starting all over again from the beginning** を直接話法に直せば、'Now, let's start all over again from the beginning.' などとなる。彼らは、実はどの時点を beginning とするつもりか？

1. 3つの箱があり、まだ選択がなされていない時点
2. 1つの箱が選ばれ、残り2つの箱はまだ開けられていない時点
3. 1つの空箱が開けられ、残り2つの箱はまだ開けられていない時点

[111] **everything that happened *before* that point:** その時点の前に起こったすべてとは、3つのうちから1つを選んだことと、残り2つのなかからハズレを排除したこと。実はこの「ハズレを排除」したことによって、第1段階と第2段階での条件が異なっている。「ハズレを排除」したため、第2段階では、「排除されなかった残り」の当たる確率が増すのである。それが everything that may happen *afterward*（l. 112）ということ。

[113] **Q. primary** の意味はどれか？

1. 原始の　　2. 最初の　　3. 最も重要な

1990年9月にアメリカのある雑誌がこの問題をとりあげて、「変更した方が、当たる確率が2倍になる」と発表したところ、博士号を持つ多数の数学者たちから「確率は2分の1だ」と強硬な反論が出るという「事件」があった。

ポール・ホフマン『放浪の天才数学者エルデシュ』平石律子訳（草思社、2000）によれば、天才数学者エルデシュも、確率は2分の1だと思ってしまった口だそうだ。

モンティ・ホール問題のおもしろさは、現実が直感と異なる場合、人は混乱するということである。本章の冒頭にあるように、人は実は理性ではなく、直感で物事をとらえていることの証左である。

さて、おまけのマンガは、「嘘つきと正直者」のパロディ。

「嘘つきと正直者」とは、「一方は天国、もう一方は地獄に続く2つの扉があり、どちらの扉にも天使がいて、どちらかは正直者で、どちらかが嘘つきである。どちらかの天使へ1回だけ質問ができ、イエスかノーかだけの答えをもらうことができる。どんな質問をするべきか」という問題のこと。

その解答はいくつか考えられる。

どちらかの天使に「天国への道の前に立っているのは、正直な天使ですか」と質問する。または、「あなたに『こちらが天国の門ですか？』とたずねたら、あなたはイエスと答えますか？」と問う、など。

ここにあるのはそのパロディで、「めんどうな質問をしたら刺すぞ」という3人目が登場する。さあ、どうする？

6

A Super Tunnel

(Part 2)

Massimo Piattelli-Palmarini

The Three Prisoners Dilemma

Here is another, older version of the three-box game.

Three prisoners face death; they are to be shot at dawn. As the next day is the birthday of the ruling tyrant, the head of the prison decides to spare one of the condemned men. He knows which he will spare, but he is a sadist and therefore decides not to reveal to any of the three prisoners the name of the man to be spared; he wants to leave them in uncertainty until the very last moment. He tells the three prisoners that one of them will certainly be spared, but that's all he tells them. He tells the prison guard who the spared prisoner will be, but enjoins the guard to keep the secret at all costs.

Filled with anguish, one of the condemned men (let's call him Prisoner C) tries to bribe the guard. He says, "As only one of us is going to be spared, it is clear that at least one of the other two of us is going to die. If you tell the name of one of those who is going to be shot for sure, I'll give you my gold watch. You're not giving away any secret, because it is mathematically certain that at least one of the other two will be shot. Just give me the name of one of the two who is certain to be shot and I'll give you this valuable watch."

The guard thinks for a moment, and then lets himself be

[5] Q. **spare** の意味はどれか？
1. 命を救う　2. 牢獄から救う　3. 後の死刑のために取っておく

[6] Q. the head of the prison が **sadist** [séidist, sǽ-] であると言われるのはなぜか？

[12] **enjoins** = orders

[12] Q. **at all costs** はどういう意味か？

[17] **for sure** = certainly

もう一つの Prisoner's Dilemma

「囚人のジレンマ」はゲーム理論でよく取り上げられる。個々の人にとっての最適の選択が、全体にとっては最適の選択とはならない状況のことである。

ある犯罪の容疑によって、2人の男が、それぞれ独房に入れられている。2人に次のような取り引きが持ちかけられた。

- 自白する場合：相棒が自白しない場合は、自分が釈放される。そして相棒は禁固10年の刑が課せられる。相棒も自白した場合は、2人とも禁固6年をくらうだろう。
- 自白しない場合：もしも相棒が自白したら、相棒は釈放される。自分は禁固10年の刑に処せられる。相棒が自白しなければ、2人とも禁固2年の刑をくらうだろう。

利己的な人間なら、どうふるまうべきだろう？ どう見ても、自白すべきことは明らかだ。自白したら、釈放か6年の刑になる。自白しなければ、2年か10年の刑に処せられるのだ。

しかし、もしも2人とも自白すると、2人の分を合わせて、のべ12年が監獄で費されることになる。これは、費される全時間という観点から見ると、最悪の結果だ。どちらも相棒を信頼して自白しないことを当てにするか泥棒にも信義がなければならないという一般原則を双方が受け入れるなら、監獄で過ごす期間はのべ4年となり時間の総計という観点からは、最良の結果となる。

日常的な状況においても、このような「囚人のジレンマ」の生じることは多いが、個々人の利己主義がつねに全体として最良の結果を生むとはかぎらないのは明らかだ。人類が生き延びることをこい願っている神がいるとすれば、人間の心の中に、せめてわずかな片隅なりとも、信頼と原則のための場所を確保しておいてくれるのではなかろうか。

（ブレンダン・ウィルソン『自分で考えてみる哲学』山本史郎訳（東京大学出版会、2004）より）

seduced. He is convinced that this will have no effect on anything; nothing is changed by telling Prisoner C. So he says, "Prisoner A will die." Prisoner C hands over his watch. He is happy because where before he had a one-in-three chance of being spared, he now has a 50/50 chance of being spared. The sacrifice of the watch is offset by his greater probability of surviving.

Question: Is Prisoner C's reasoning correct?

Gloss: If it was already certain that (at least) one of the other two must die, how is it possible that just knowing which of the other two will die will improve Prisoner C's chances of surviving? Isn't that magic? I invite the reader to put down his book and think out his own answer to this enigma.

The correct reply is as follows: Prisoner C's chance of being spared is and remains one in three, but, thanks to the information provided by the guard, the probability of the remaining prisoner, Prisoner B, being spared has now risen to 66 percent, or a two-thirds probability.

Prisoner C has strayed into one of our mental tunnels; he has fallen into a probability trap. The only one who gains from his sacrifice of his gold watch is Prisoner B, who may know nothing at all about the transaction and has been sleeping in his cell. If it seems to you quite mad that Prisoner B's chances of survival have objectively increased, thanks to something that happened in which he took no part and of which he knows nothing, then yours is a cognitive illusion. An increased probability is not a sort of "fluid" that can pass in a jolt from one prisoner to another and produce a material change.

In the three-box problem, we dislike the idea that the chances of a box containing the money can augment or diminish while that box remains closed, inert, and intact, without anything having been added to or taken away from it. That is the same illusion. We dislike the idea that Prisoner B's chances of survival have been increased by an event in which the beneficiary took no part, and about which he knows nothing. Symmetrically, we dislike the idea that the chances of Prisoner C, who has elicited

[26] **where** = whereas (although).
Cf. Thinking that you understand when in fact you don't is a great error.

[28] **is offset by . . . :** ～で埋め合わせができる (is compensated by)

[31] **Gloss:** 注解。しばしば欄外に記されたものを指す。

[35] **think out:** 考え出す。とことん考えて結論を出すというニュアンス。
Cf. He worked out the answer to the question by himself.

[35] **enigma** [əníɡmə, in-, ɛn-]: 謎

[44] Q. **the transaction** はどういう意味か？

[48] Q. **yours** = your opinion that it is (　　　)

[48] **yours is a cognitive illusion** = you have fallen into a cognitive illusion.

[48] **cognitive illusion:** 認識上の錯覚。Cf. p. 36, l. 1.
Cf. optical illusion 視覚的錯覚。

[49] **in a jolt** [dʒóult]: ドックンと（急に「液体」が流れるさま）

[50] **material change:** 実質的・物質的な変化

[52] Q. **augment** と同じ意味合いの語を同じ段落から選びなさい。

[53] Q. **inert** [inə́ːrt] の意味はどれか？
1. 動かない　2. 不活性の　3. 活動的でない

[53] **intact** [intǽkt] = untouched

[56] Q. **the beneficiary** とは誰か？

[57] Q. **Symmetrically** の意味はどちらか？
1. その反面　2. それと同じように

and received the piece of information, have not changed at all. It is our view of what a probability is that betrays us. We think of probability not as an abstract mathematical entity but as a "thing," a "process"; to us it has real weight and body.

The objective probability of an event involving any given individual may well be affected by another event taking place anywhere in the world, and quite without that individual knowing about it. Prisoner C thinks his chances of survival have jumped from one-third to one-half because he suffers from the same illusion we saw in the three-box problem: He believes that in any given situation about whose outcome he is uncertain, probability is subdivided equally and becomes 50/50. But here again, the only link that rigorous probability calculation allows is that the sum of two probabilities is 1, or 100 percent; probability theory does not claim that this sum is necessarily equally divided between the two remaining boxes, or the two undesignated prisoners.

There is an elegant reasoning that also shows the absurdity of Prisoner C's argument, and why his probability of survival cannot be improved. Suppose the guard says it is Prisoner B rather than Prisoner A who is sure to die.

This would make no difference at all to Prisoner C, because all he wants, following his strange way of thinking, is to rule out one of the other two as certainly condemned. Any one of the other two will do for him. In fact, the subjectively experienced boost in probability, from one-third to one-half, is tied for him to the certainty that now there are only two candidates left who could possibly benefit from pardon. Therefore, as it does not matter at all to him which prisoner is actually named by the guard, and because he knows for sure that at least one of them will die, he may as well toss a coin himself and pick one of the other two at random. In other words, he may as well imagine that there is a guard whom he manages to bribe. All this rigmarole might as well take place in the private chamber of his own imagination.

Thus Prisoner C can self-boost his chances from one-third to one-half. If, I say if, we assume that the line of reasoning of

[61] Q. **an abstract mathematical entity** = something that has no real (　　　) or (　　　)

[63] **The objective probability:** 推測（guesses, inferences）や自分なりの見積もり（subjective assessments）ではなく、事実や実験等に基づく確率。

[63] **given:** 所与の

[64] **may well be affected** = has a good chance of being affected

[70] **subdivided:** 囚人Aがもっていた3分の1の確率が、囚人BとCのあいだで再配分されると考える。BとCのどちらが死ぬかわからないのだから、等分すればfifty-fiftyだと囚人Cは考えている。しかし実際には、ここにモンティ・ホール問題が生じる。囚人Bは、死ぬ人として（とりあえずは）選ばれなかったという付加条件があるので、囚人Cより助かる確率が高いのである。

[71] **rigorous:** 正確な、厳密な

[74] Q. **undesignated prisoners** の意味はどれか？

1. 無名の囚人
2. 誰と特定されていない囚人
3. 死刑になると言われていない囚人

[82] Q. **Any one . . . will do for him** の意味はどれか？

1. どちらでも彼を殺すことになる
2. 彼にとっては、どちらでもかまわない
3. どちらにしても彼は死刑の宣言を受ける

[83] **the subjectively experienced boost in probability** = the rise in probability he subjectively experienced

[86] Q. **pardon** の内容を説明している語句を本文中より探しなさい。

[89] **may as well toss a coin . . . and pick . . . :** コインでも投げて〜を選んでもよい（同じことだ）。had better がかなり強い命令口調であるのに対して、それよりは柔らかく勧める表現。

[92] **rigmarole** [rígmərὸul]: くだらない長話

[92] **might as well take place in . . . :** 〜で起きたとしても同じことだ。might（may）as well A as B は、AとBにほとんど違いがないことを示す。上記注[89]、および You might as well throw your money away as lend it to him（彼に金を貸すのは捨てるようなものだ）などの表現を参照のこと。might を使うと may より現実味が薄くなる。

[92] **chamber** [tʃéimbə(r)] = room

[94] Q. **self-boost** の意味はどちらか？

1. 自分が助かる確率を引き上げる　　2. 確率を自分勝手に引き上げる

Prisoner C is probabilistically right, then he has a one-half (50 percent) chance of being saved. But then an identical piece of reasoning is open to any one of the three prisoners. Thus each of them would have a probability of one-half (or 50 percent) of being saved. This is, of course, a monstrosity from the point of [100]
view of the most basic probability theory: Their cumulative probabilities would add up to more than 100 percent (in fact, to 150 percent). This is a little proof per absurdum that shows that the reasoning of Prisoner C cannot be right.

[96] **probabilistically:** 確率論的に（=by the use of the probability theory 確率論の使用によって）。Cf. l. 101.

[100] Q. **monstrosity** はどういう意味か？

[101] **cumulative** [kjúːmjulətiv, -lèi-]: 累積の

[102] **add up to . . . :** 合計して〜になる

[103] **proof per absurdum** = reductio ad absurdum【論理】背理法。ある命題を真と仮定し、それを基にした推論が不合理になることを立証することにより、最初の命題が偽であることを示す方法。

7

The Pendulum Clock of Christiaan Huygens

(Part 1)

Lisa Jardine

The Pepys Library

Sometimes if you are lucky as an historian, you find a bit of evidence which illuminates a big idea. That happened to me in the Pepys Library at Magdalene College, Cambridge, in April 2006, when I made a discovery which allowed me to correct the historical record. It concerned a piece of documentary evidence repeatedly used to prove that a Dutch scientist had been the first to invent a clock accurate enough to determine the precise position of a ship on the open sea.

The manuscript I found in Cambridge was a ship's journal kept by a seventeenth-century English sea-captain, who had offered to give space on his ship for some state-of-the-art scientific equipment—two new pendulum clocks—on a voyage to

[About the Author]

Lisa Jardine: リサ・ジャーディーン（1944–2015）。歴史家、シェイクスピア学者。ロンドン大学クィーン・メアリー・コレッジ教授。著作に *Still Harping on Daughters: Women and Drama in the Age of Shakespeare*（1983）や *Reading Shakespeare Historically*（1996）などがある。本章は、BBC 4 のラジオ番組 'A Point of View' で著者が話した原稿に基づいている *A Point of View*（London: Preface Publishing, 2008）からの一節。

[Title] **Pendulum:** 振り子

[Title] **Christiaan Huygens** [háigənz, hɔ́i-]**:** クリスティアーン・ホイヘンス（1629–95）。オランダの数学者・物理学者・天文学者。1655 年、土星の環を認識、翌年に振り子時計を世界で初めて製作した。1678 年にホイヘンスの原理（波動の基本原理）を発見し、光の波動説を唱えた。

Christiaan Huygens

[1] **an historian:** イギリス英語では historian, historic, historical, hotel といった単語に不定冠詞の an をつけ、語頭にある h を発音しないことがある（いずれも h の直後に第 1 アクセントがない単語）。ただし、今日では古風な発音である。

[2] **Q. illuminates** の意味はどれか？
1. 輝かす　　2. 啓蒙する　　3. 明らかにする

[3] **the Pepys** [píːps] **Library:** ケンブリッジ大学モードリン・コレッジに、サミュエル・ピープス（63 ページ注 [53] を参照）が自らの膨大な日記と蔵書を 1703 年に寄贈したことによって作られた文庫。

[3] **Magdalene** [mɔ́ːdlən] **College:** イギリスのケンブリッジ大学を構成するコレッジ（学寮）の一つ。1428 年に創設され、1542 年に現在の名前となる。

[8] **open sea:** 外海、外洋（陸地に囲まれていない、大きく広がった海域）

[9] **ship's journal:** 航海日誌

[11] **state-of-the-art:** 最新の

the west coast of Africa and back. The job he agreed to undertake for the recently founded Royal Society was to test the clocks at regular intervals on his journey, to see if they kept accurate time in spite of being tossed up and down and generally shaken about at sea.

The thought uppermost in my mind as I worked my way through the manuscript materials in the library was how odd it is that non-scientists think of science as being concerned with certainties and absolute truth. Because in fact the contrary is the case: scientists are on the whole quite tentative about their results. They simply try to arrive at the best fit between the experimental findings so far and a general principle.

Science is not doctrinaire. Strongly held religious beliefs, however, are. In the same week that I was transcribing seventeenth-century handwritten records in Cambridge, John Mackay from Queensland, Australia, an extreme advocate of Creationism, was touring halls and chapels in the UK attacking Darwin's theory that the human race has evolved gradually from the apes over millions of years. Mackay is one of those who maintain that Genesis is literally true, that the earth is a mere 6000 years old, and that the exquisite organisation of nature is clear proof that God's hand lies behind all of creation. During his visit Mackay had hoped to debate the matter with leading British scientists. If evolution is 'true', the Creationist challenges, step up and prove it.

There is something rather attractive about absolute beliefs. Most of us find the idea of certainty comforting: 'The sun will rise tomorrow'. Uncertainty, on the other hand, is much more unsettling.

One of the reasons why we find it difficult to make up our minds about climate change and global warming is that the data are so complicated. Glaciers are melting, holes are detected in the ozone layer, emission of greenhouse gases is rising, yet we have just gone through an unusually cold winter, spring is unseasonably late arriving and it seems to have been raining continuously for months—it is hard to get alarmed. Scientists tell us that analysis of the current experimental data suggests

[14] **the Royal Society:** 王立協会。世界で最も古い科学アカデミー。1660年に私的組織として設立され、1662年に国王に認可された。初期の会長としては建築家のクリストファー・レン、サミュエル・ピープス、科学者アイザック・ニュートンらが名を連ねている。

[18] **uppermost in my mind:** 第一に念頭にある

[18] **worked my way through . . . :**「動詞＋one's way＋前置詞」は「努力して持続的動作を行う」という意味の定型表現。Cf. I shouldered my way through the crowd. 私は肩で押しながら群衆を通り抜けた。/ I read my way through the library. 私はその図書館の本を読み尽くした。

[21] **Q. . . . is the case** の意味はどれか？
1. 〜が事実である　2. 〜は事件である
3. 〜はケース・バイ・ケースである

[22] **Q. tentative** の意味はどれか？
1. ためらいを示す　2. 曖昧な姿勢を見せる
3. 仮のものという態度をとる

[23] **Q. the best fit between . . . principle** の意味はどちらか？
1. 実験等で得られた資料に最も合致する理論は何かを考える
2. 実験等で発見されたことと一般原則との最も適した融合をはかる

[25] **Q. doctrinaire** とは、この文脈では、どんな意味か？

[28] **Q. advocate** の意味はどれか？　1. 弁護士　2. 擁護する者　3. 創始者

[28] **Creationism:** 創造説。聖書の天地創造は真実であるとし、世界は現在の形に神が創造したと唱える考え方。対立概念は Evolutionism である。

[32] **Genesis:** 聖書の「創世記」

[32] **Q. literally** の反意語はどれか？
1. artificially　2. scientifically　3. metaphorically

[32] **a mere 6000 years old:** ほんの6000年前にできた。a mere 6000 years のように、「a(n)＋形容詞＋数詞＋複数名詞」を組み合わせることは珍しくない。E.g. The price is an astonishing 100,000 dollars. / I had an enjoyable two weeks in London. 複数名詞の前に不定冠詞が用いられるのは、「数詞＋複数名詞」が一つの集合体としてとらえられているため。

[36] **Q. step up** の意味はどれか？ Cf. speak up.
1. 進歩する　2. 堂々と前に出る　3. グレードアップする

[41] **Q. unsettling** の同義語はどれか？
1. confusing　2. surprising　3. disturbing

[42] **Q. make up our minds** の意味はどれか？
1. 決意する　2. 考えを決める　3. 心を入れ替える

[44] **Glaciers:** 氷河

[45] **greenhouse gases:** 温室効果ガス。京都議定書では削減対象として、二酸化炭素、メタン、CFC（フロン）など6種類の温室効果ガスが定められている。

that over the next 90 years sea-levels are likely to rise well over 10 centimetres—which means that entire coastlines will disappear. But even a passionate advocate of the prospect of impending ecological disaster like the Prime Minister's scientific advisor Sir David King cannot, as a scientist, go so far as to say, 'It will be so. That is the absolute truth of the matter'. Instead TV and the newspapers offer us extensive coverage of the ecological scientists' warnings and doom-laden predictions, and we have to make up our own minds.

It is a basic requirement of scientific method that a tentative explanation has to be tested against observation of the natural world. From the very beginning scientists have been suspicious whenever the data fit the hoped-for results too closely.

Which brings me back to my clock-testing sea-captain, and the ship's journal I was reading in Cambridge. I was looking for documents relating to attempts by the seventeenth-century Dutch scientist Christiaan Huygens to develop a pendulum clock which would enable mariners to find their longitude at sea (their precise east-west position on the surface of the globe).

Huygens's pendulum clock (replica)

[50] **well:** 十分に、かなり ⇒ **well over . . . :** 優に〜以上

[54] **Sir David King:** 1939年生まれの南アフリカ出身の化学者。2000年から2007年にかけて、トニー・ブレアおよびゴードン・ブラウン政権下でイギリス政府の主席科学顧問（Chief Scientific Adviser）を務め、気候変動に関して警鐘を鳴らした。

[56] **coverage:** 報道

[57] **doom-laden:** 世界の終末（破滅）を告げる。〜-laden は「〜をぎっしり積んだ」、「〜に満ちた」。99ページ注[75]参照。

[59] **Q. a tentative explanation** と対立的な概念を表している表現を、前の段落から指摘しなさい。

[60] **Q. be tested against . . .** はどういう意味か？

[61] **Q. From the very beginning** は、この文脈では何を意味しているか？

[67] **longitude:** 経度。経度測定の難しさについては、デーヴァ・ソベル『経度への挑戦』藤井留美訳、角川文庫（角川書店、2010）を参照。
Cf. latitude 緯度。

正確に経度を測定することで、地球上の現在地を正しく把握することは、未知の海域への探検航海をはじめ、科学的にも軍事的にもきわめて重要な問題であったが、18世紀初頭、正確にこの経度を測定することはまだできずにいた。（ちなみに緯度は、太陽の南中時の角度を計測することで分かるので、古代からかなり正確に理解されていた。）経度を正確に測るには、例えば赤道上の海洋であれば、船の速度から移動距離を算出し、それと赤道全体の長さの比を求めればよい。（なお、今日では経度の基準、すなわち経度ゼロはロンドンのグリニッジ子午線と定められているが、これが世界各国で採用されたのは19世紀後半のことであって、18世紀には、船の出港地などを適宜経度ゼロの基準と定めて位置を表記することが一般的だった。）しかしこの場合、船の速度を正確に測るための精密時計（クロノメーター）が必要になる。なにしろ、例えば赤道上であれば、30秒の誤差はおよそ1キロの差にもなるからだ。ところがこの精密時計が、18世紀初頭にはまだなかった。そこでイギリス議会は、1714年、正確な経度測定に成功した者に賞金1万ポンド（のち、2万ポンドに増額）を授与するとの議決をし、経度測定委員会が発足した。この難題を解決したのは、精密時計開発の父とされる時計師ジョン・ハリソン（John Harrison, 1693–1776）だった。1762年に彼の時計の正確さは立証されたが、庶民出身の技術者だったハリソンへの偏見もあり、賞金は一部しか授与されなかった。ただし1773年にイギリス議会はハリソンの功績を認め、8750ポンドを授与した。

原田範行「かなたに何かある」（石原保徳・原田範行『新しい世界への旅立ち』シリーズ世界周航記別巻〔岩波書店、2006〕所収）より一部改変。

About Huygens's Pendulum Clock

by Brendan Wilson

The pendulum clock was invented by Christiaan Huygens (1629–1695), a Dutch astronomer, mathematician, physicist and inventor who was one of the leading scientists of his time. But how did the pendulum clock work?

The time taken for a pendulum to swing from one extreme to the other and back (its period) depends on the width of the swing (the amplitude): a longer swing takes more time. However, Galileo discovered—sometime around 1600—that as long as the amplitude is kept small, changes in amplitude have no significant effect on period. He realised that this would make a small-amplitude pendulum useful as a time-keeper, and he designed (but never built) a clock based on this idea.

In 1656, Huygens actually built a clock which used a controlled-amplitude pendulum to regulate its action. The result was a huge increase in accuracy, from about 15 minutes error per day, to about 15 seconds. (Until about 1670, clocks did not have a minute hand—there was no point.)

This improved accuracy had many important consequences of course, but one dramatic result was a proof that the earth is not spherical. In 1671, a French astronomer noticed that his clock ran more than 2 minutes slower in Cayenne, near the equator, than in Paris. He inferred that the local strength of gravity was weaker at Cayenne. Then in 1687, Newton showed that this is because the earth is oblate (flattened at the poles), due to the centrifugal force of rotation. At the equator, we are further from the centre of the earth, and therefore less subject to its gravity.

So improved understanding of pendulum movement led to more accurate clocks, which led to a proof that the earth rotates! Truly a wonderful example of the mutually reinforcing discoveries of the Scientific Revolution.

[77] **amplitude:**【物理】振幅。ガリレオの発見したいわゆる「振り子の等時性」は、本文にあるとおりこの振幅が小さいときにのみ成立する。ガリレオについては、137 ページ注 [45] 参照。

[87] Q. **there was no point** = there was no point in having a (　　) (　　)

[91] **Cayenne:** カイエンヌ。南アメリカの北東岸にある港町。現在はフランス領ギアナの県都。

[94] **oblate** [óbleit | ɑ́b-]: 上下の両極で扁平な

[95] Q. **we are . . . less subject to its gravity** = gravity is

1. weaker　2. about equal　3. stronger

[99] Q. **mutually reinforcing discoveries** とはどのようなことか？

[100] **Scientific Revolution:** 科学革命。17 世紀西欧にガリレイやニュートンらの科学者によって古典力学の基礎が確立され、それにともなって自然像・世界像に大変革が生じた現象。

氷河が溶けると海水面が上昇するのみならず、氷から氷へ泳ぎ渡るホッキョクグマの居場所がなくなることも意味する。現在、国際自然保護連合（IUCN = International Union for Conservation of Natural Resources）は、ホッキョクグマを絶滅の可能性がある危急種（VU = vulnerable species）に指定している。

8

The Pendulum Clock of Christiaan Huygens

(Part 2)

Lisa Jardine

In 1664, shortly after the first proper scientific research institute, the Royal Society, had been established in London, its President, who was an admirer of Huygens's work, offered to organise a series of sea-trials to be conducted by the English navy, using two of his pioneering clocks. Precise locating of a ship's position at sea was absolutely crucial for naval warfare, as well as for ensuring that they could navigate clear of rocks and shoals. Captain Robert Holmes, commander in charge of the Navy ship the *Jersey*, agreed to take the clocks along with him on a six-month voyage down the west coast of Africa. He would keep the clocks wound and in working order, take regular measurements, make the necessary complex calculations, and supply detailed documentation in support of his findings.

When he got back to London in 1665 Holmes presented his report to an expectant Royal Society. The clocks had performed spectacularly well. Indeed, he declared, they had actually saved the expedition from disaster. On the return journey, Holmes had been obliged to sail several hundred nautical miles westwards in order to pick up a favourable wind. Having done so, the *Jersey* and the three ships accompanying her sailed several hundred more miles north-eastwards. At which point, the four captains found that water was running worryingly low on board. Holmes's three fellow-captains produced three competing sets of calculations of their current position based on traditional

[1] Q. **proper** の意味はどれか？
1. 厳密な　2. 礼儀正しい　3. ちゃんとした、本物の

[4] Q. **sea-trials** とは何か？

[5] Q. **pioneering** の意味はどれか？
1. 先駆的な　2. 辺境旅行者用の　3. 先駆者にふさわしい

[6] **naval warfare:** 海上戦

[7] **navigate clear of . . . :** ～を避けて航行する

[7] **shoals** [ʃóulz]**:** 浅瀬

[8] **Robert Holmes:** ロバート・ホームズ（Sir ～、*c.* 1622–92）。のちに英国海軍の提督。

[8] **commander:** 艦長。18 世紀以降、イギリス海軍（Royal Navy）では、大砲を 20 門以上装備していた軍艦の艦長は captain、小艦（sloop）の艦長は commander というのが正式名称となっていった（ただし、日常的な呼称としてはどちらも captain）。

[8] **in charge of . . . :** ～を指揮している

[10] Q. **He would keep . . .** = He said, ‘I (　　　) keep . . . ’

[11] **in working order:**（機械などが）正常に動く状態にある

[11] Q. **take regular measurements** はどういう意味か？

[18] **nautical miles:** 海里（現在では約 1852 m。1929 年以前のイギリスでは約 1853 m。なお、陸上の mile は約 1609 m。）

[19] **favourable wind:** 順風。Cf. favourable opportunity 好機。

[22] Q. **water was running worryingly low on board** はどういう意味か？

[23] Q. **competing sets of calculations** はどういう意味か？

reckoning, but all agreed that they were dangerously far from any potential source of water. Not so, declared Holmes. According to his calculations—based on the pendulum clocks—they were a mere 90 miles west of the island of Fuego, one of the Cape Verde islands. He persuaded the party to set their course due east—whereupon, the very next day, around noon, they indeed made landfall on Fuego, exactly as predicted.

London was abuzz with excitement. The Fellows of the Royal Society were elated, and immediately rushed Holmes's account of how the pendulum clocks had saved the day into print. Orders began to be placed for the revolutionary new timekeepers.

But the inventor himself, Christiaan Huygens, was not so sure. And his reason for being more cautious than his London colleagues was precisely the fact that the clocks had proved so astonishingly accurate:

'I have to confess', he wrote to the Royal Society, 'that I had not expected such a spectacular result from these clocks'.

And he went on: 'I beg you to tell me if the said Captain seems a sincere man whom one can absolutely trust. For it must be said that I am amazed that the clocks were sufficiently accurate to allow him by their means to locate such a tiny island'.

Well, Robert Holmes was not 'a sincere man'. In fact, he was a rather notorious rogue. History remembers him as the man whose thuggish and piratical behaviour towards the Dutch merchants along the Guinea coast in the 1660s directly caused the second Anglo-Dutch war.

So the Royal Society asked an official from the Navy Board, Samuel Pepys—the same Pepys who wrote the diary—to check the evidence Holmes had provided against the day-by-day entries in his ship's journal. Pepys went off somewhat reluctantly to dine with Holmes—he confessed that he was rather afraid of him. Well, that was the journal I went to look at in Cambridge. Lo and behold! It turns out that Holmes had greatly exaggerated. The pendulum clocks had proved no more accurate for calculating longitude than conventional methods; the ships had been well and truly lost; the mariners had been extremely lucky

[25] **reckoning:**【海】（天文観測による）船位の算出。

[26] Q. **potential source of water** はどういう意味か？

[28] **the island of Fuego:** フエゴ島、あるいはフォゴ（Fogo）島。西アフリカのセネガル西方海上にあるカーボヴェルデ諸島（Cape Verde Islands 右下地図参照）の南部に位置する。フエゴ島はスペイン語名だが、カーボヴェルデ諸島全体が 1975 年までポルトガル領であったため、通常はポルトガル語名のフォゴ島が用いられる。fuego も fogo も「火」を意味し、フォゴ島全体が活火山である。

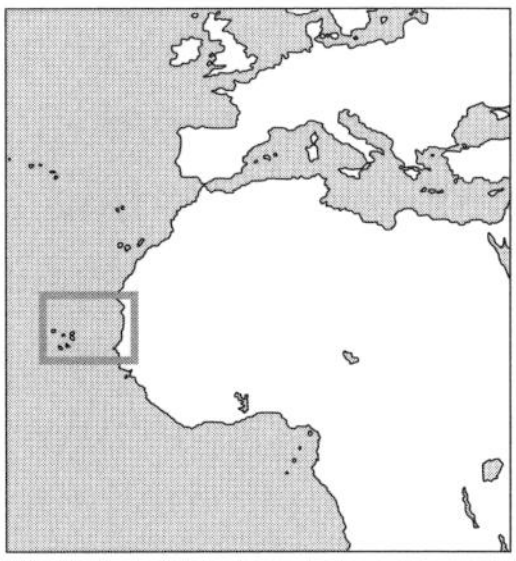

Cape Verde Islands

[29] Q. **the party** はどういう意味か？

[30] **due east:** 真東

[30] **whereupon:** それから、その結果

[31] **landfall:**（船の）陸地接近、上陸

[32] **abuzz** [əbʌ́z]:（興奮などで）沸き立っている

[33] Q. **rushed . . . into print** はどういう意味か？

[34] **saved the day:** 困難を救った

[35] Q. **Orders began to be placed for . . .** はどういう意味か？

[35] Q. **timekeepers** の意味はどれか？
1. 時計　　2. 記録保持者　　3. 記録計測係

[38] Q. **cautious** は何について「用心深い」のか？

[43] **said:** 上記の、前述の

[46] Q. **by their means** はどういう意味か？

[49] **thuggish** ⇐ thug 暴漢、殺し屋

[49] **piratical** ⇐ pirate 海賊

[50] **Guinea** [gíni]: ギニア（アフリカ西部の沿岸地方）。かつてヨーロッパ諸国の奴隷貿易の拠点だった。

[51] **Anglo-Dutch war:** 英蘭戦争。17 世紀後半、イギリスとオランダは第 1 回（1652–54）、第 2 回（1665–67）、第 3 回（1672–74）と、3 度戦争をした。

[52] **Navy Board:** 英国海軍の中の、艦隊を管理する部門。

[53] **Samuel Pepys:** サミュエル・ピープス（1633–1705）。1660 年から 1669 年にかけて王政復古期の世相について史的価値の高い日記を遺したことで知られているが、官僚として海軍再建などにも功績があった。

[57] **the journal I went to look at in Cambridge:** 52 ページ 9 行目参照。

[58] **Lo and behold!:** 見よ！（驚きを表す古い言い回しだが、今日ではおどけて発せられる、滑稽感をともなった表現）

[61] **well and truly:** 文字どおりには「立派に正しく」。「まさしく」という意味の誇張表現。

to make landfall on the island of Saint Vincent several days after they turned back eastwards, just before their water entirely ran out.

Holmes thought that by tampering with his evidence he would please the scientists at the Royal Society. Instead, the too-precise nature of the match between his data and the results they wanted alerted them to the fact that his testimony was unreliable. And Huygens was right to be sceptical. His pendulum clocks never did prove accurate enough at sea to solve the problem of finding longitude.

A scrupulous scientist like Huygens would rather be disappointed than accept dubious evidence to provide pat confirmation of a pet theory.

And that continues to be true in all areas of scientific investigation today. Which is why no scientist would take up the Creationist Mackay's challenge to 'prove' the truth of Darwin's theory of evolution in a public debate. They knew they could not present a strongly held view based on a body of supporting evidence with the absolute certainty of a revealed truth. The most today's Royal Society was prepared to say was that a belief that all species on Earth have always existed in their present form, and that the Earth was formed in 4000 BC was 'not consistent with the evidence from geology, astronomy and physics'.

And that is probably not enough to satisfy ordinary thoughtful citizens without a scientific training, because most of us want certainty. It makes us feel safe. We're on the side of the seventeenth-century ship's captain, believing the experiments ought to prove the scientific theory once and for all.

Unfortunately, where arguments about ecology are concerned, time is not on our side. We cannot afford ourselves the luxury of waiting for evidence which clinches the theory. We are going to have to learn how to participate in debates which are not about certainties. We are going to have to get used to asking ourselves questions in the form: Is this theory consistent with the evidence currently available? A public understanding of science has never been more important.

[62] **the island of Saint Vincent:** サン・ヴィセンテ島。カーボヴェルデ諸島の北部に位置する。

[65] Q. **tamper with** の意味はどれか？

1. 改変する　2. 追加する　3. もみ消す

[68] **alerted** someone **to** = made someone aware of

[73] **pat:** ぴったりの（しばしば「都合が良すぎる」といった意味で否定的に用いる。）

E.g. The ending of the novel is a little too pat to be convincing.

[74] Q. **pet** の意味はどれか？

1. small　2. pretty　3. favourite

[80] Q. **The most today's Royal Society was prepared to say was** の文法構造を明らかにしなさい。

[81] Q. **a belief** の内容を示しているのは、どこからどこまでか？

[83] **not consistent with the evidence from . . . :**「〜から得られる証拠とは相容れない」という意味の決まり文句

[87] Q. **training** の意味はどれか？

1. 教育　2. 技能訓練　3. トレーニング

[90] Q. **once and for all** の意味はどれか？

1. 一度きり　2. きっぱりと　3. 皆のために決定的に

[92] Q. ここは熟語表現 'time is on our side' に基づいているが、この熟語表現はどういう意味か？

[93] Q. **clinches the theory** の意味はどれか？

1. 理論をねじ曲げる
2. 理論について議論し合う
3. 理論を決定的なものにする

[96] **consistent with . . . :**「〜と一致する」より、「〜と矛盾しない」と訳したほうが原語のニュアンスが出る。

[97] Q. **A public understanding of science has never been more important.**

= It is more important that ordinary people today should understand the nature of（　　）than at any（　　）time in history.

Personally, I am absolutely certain that a literal belief in a unique and perfect moment of Creation, presided over by an omniscient Deity, is no help in making important decisions concerning the here-and-now—like whether we should sacrifice our right to cut-price air-travel around the globe in order significantly to cut carbon emissions. At this crossroads in our planet's history, faith is no foundation for understanding slow and incremental climatic change, and the increasing likelihood that the human race faces an imperfect ecological future.

[100] Q. **unique** の意味はどれか？

1. 独特の、他に類を見ない
2. 唯一の、一度きりの
3. ちょっと変わった、ユニークな

[101] **omniscient** = knowing everything

[101] **Deity** = God

[103] Q. **cut-price air-travel** はどういう意味か？

[104] Q. **crossroads** の意味はどちらか？

1. 十字路、交差点、道が直角に交わるところ
2. 分岐点、重大決意をすべき岐路

[106] **incremental** = ever-increasing

9

The Secret Garden

(Part 1)

John D. Barrow

A typical African savannah landscape

The fact that our ancestors spent very long periods in tropical savannah habitats leads us to expect that some of our emotional responses to such an environment may possess adaptive features. Instinctive aesthetic reactions to the world could not have evolved if, on average, they contributed negatively to survival. By contrast, those responses that enhance the chances of survival will persist. They provide us with important clues to the source of our most basic aesthetic preferences.

The relative longevity of early humans ensured that they would need various habitats to maintain a life-long supply of resources. Their mobility allowed them to meet that need. Indeed, studies show that early hunter-gatherers moved

[About the Author]

John D. Barrow: ジョン・D・バロウ（1952–2020）。イギリスの数学者・物理学者。ケンブリッジ大学教授。一般向けの科学啓蒙書の執筆も多数ある。本章は、*The Artful Universe*（1995; 2nd ed., Oxford: Oxford University Press, 2011）からの一節。

[2] **savannah:** サバンナ。広大で木の少ない草原地。

[2] **habitats** = places to live in

[3] **adaptive features:**「適応性のある特徴」と辞書どおりに訳すだけでは本当に意味がわかったことにならない。この adaptive は、自然環境に適合する特徴を備えた個体が生き残り（survive）、種の中で支配的になっていくというダーウィンの進化論における「自然選択」（natural selection）——15 行目に出てくる——という概念を背景としており、その文脈から「自然環境に適応し、生き残りを可能にするような」という意味で理解しなければならない。

[4] **Q. Instinctive aesthetic reactions** とは何か？

1. 美学へと向かう本能　　2. 何かを美しいと感じる本能的な心の動き

[5] **Q. they** は何を指すか？

[5] **Q. contributed negatively to survival** はどういう意味か？

[7] **Q. persist** の意味はどれか？

1. 固執する　　2. 残る、存続する　　3. 主張する

[2] **The relative longevity of early humans** = the fact that early humans lived longer than (　　　)(　　　)

[11] **Q. Their mobility** はどういう意味か？

[12] **hunter-gatherers:**（動物の）狩猟や（果実・木の実などの）採取で生きていた者たち

frequently. The mobility of humans ensures that they will need to make choices about the best environment; the criteria used to make those choices will inevitably be acted upon by natural selection over very long periods of time. Small organisms that are short-lived, or fixed in space, or moved aimlessly by winds and water currents, or limited in their foraging ranges, will not encounter the problem of environmental choice.

The habitat in which humans originated was that of a tropical African savannah. It is therefore possible that we have developed preferences for environments with many of the characteristic, life-enhancing features that this habitat offered during the Pleistocene era. These will have interesting aesthetic byproducts because our ancestors did not have direct access to some infallible measure of the safety, or the fertility, of a particular environment. They did not take soil samples or monitor the crime levels. All they could do was examine a variety of indicators correlated to the fitness of the environment in their experience—experience that valued safety and survival. Similarly, when birds explore potential nesting sites in woodland, they need to be sensitive to a variety of factors concerning the availability of food and security, but ornithologists have discovered that they make their decisions about whether to nest in a particular site on the basis of the abundance and pattern of tree branchings. It is likely that some human choices of suitable habitats were made in response to easily accessible cues, in a similar way.

Psychologists have carried out a number of controlled experiments on children and adults to discover which environments they prefer. By using photographs it is possible to remove extraneous factors (like the presence of water or animals) and to expose the viewers to habitats of which they have had no direct experience. The results are interesting. It is found that among very young children the savannah environment was the most preferred. (The desert was preferred the least.) But older teenagers, who had experienced other environments (like deciduous woodland, rainforests), often liked them just as much as the savannah. When experience is limited and the subjects are

[14] **criteria** ⇐ criterion [kraitíəriən] の複数形

[15] **be acted upon by . . .** = be influenced by . . .

[18] **foraging** [fɔ́(ː)ridʒiŋ] = searching for food or provisions

[23] Q. **this habitat** とは何か？

[24] **the Pleistocene** [pláistousìːn | pláistə-] **era:** 更新（洪積）世。地球の表面に広く氷河が発達していた時代。人は更新世のサバンナで進化したのであり、マット・リドレー『やわらかな遺伝子』中村桂子・斉藤隆央訳（紀伊國屋書店、2004）によれば、「人間の意識は、都会というジャングルではなく、更新世のサバンナに合うように作られている」。

[24] Q. **These** はどの語を指しているか？

1. preferences　2. environments　3. features

[24] Q. **by-products** は、この文脈では、どんな意味になるか？

[26] **infallible** = absolutely trustworthy or sure

[27] **monitor**（v.）= watch and check something over a period of time

[31] **potential nesting sites:** 巣作りに適した場所

[32] **sensitive to** = acutely aware of

[33] **ornithologists:** 鳥類学者

[37] Q. **cue(s)** は本来舞台用語で、俳優の動きやセリフ、効果音や照明の変化などのきっかけを意味するが、ここではどのような意味で用いられているのだろうか？

[39] **controlled experiments:** 比較対照群をきちんと設定して行われる実験

[41] **extraneous** [ikstréiniəs] = irrelevant

[47] **deciduous** [disídjuəs | -sídʒu-]**:** 落葉性の

[49] **subjects:** 被験者

choosing from photographs of environments of which they lack experience, then the savannah landscape is the most pleasing. This provides evidence for an innate bias towards the savannah habitat that, in the absence of overriding experiences of other conditions, creates a natural aesthetic disposition as a legacy of the adaptive success of our early ancestors.

The savannah landscape is an environment with many reliable cues for safe and fruitful human habitation. These cues are widely reproduced in our parklands and recreation areas (see the picture below). There is scattered tree cover, which offers shade and escape from ferocious predators, interspersed with grasses; yet there are long vistas with frequent undulations that allow good views, orientation, and way-finding. Most food sources are within a metre or two of the ground, whereas in a forested environment life is concentrated, out of reach, high above the ground, and terrestrial creatures are condemned to scavenge for the scraps that fall from the forest canopy. The most distinctive unpredictability about savannah life is the availability of water. The presence of trees, greenery, and water therefore offers an instant evaluation of the suitability of a potential habitat. These primary indicators, together with a sense of the openness of the terrain, its prospects for shelter, and the furtive viewing of others, are valuable sensitivities that signal whether further exploration or settlement can safely ensue.

A savannah-like landscape
Richmond Park, London, first enclosed by King Charles I in 1637

[52] **Q. innate bias towards the savannah habitat** の意味はどれか？
1. サバンナへの本質的な偏り
2. サバンナへの本能的な好み
3. サバンナへの生まれつきの偏見

[53] **overriding experiences of other conditions** = experiences of other conditions that override instinctive reactions

[53] **Q. overriding** の意味はどれか？
1. 先行する　2. 重なり合う　3. 無効にする

[58] **parklands:**（イギリスの）大邸宅の周囲の（広大な）庭園

[60] **predators** = animals that kill and eat other animals

[61] **long vistas:** vista は、並木のあいだなど、限られた視界から遠くを眺めるときの眺めを言う。類似語の view は「眺め」を意味する一般的な語で、prospect はある地点から広く開けた「展望」。

[61] **undulations:**（地面の）起伏

[62] **Q. orientation** = sense of (　　　)

[63] **Q. within a metre or two of the ground** の意味はどれか？
1. 地面から高さ 1、2 m 以内で　2. 半径 1、2 m の地面の範囲内で

[63] **Q. a forested environment** はどういう意味か？

[64] **Q. life is concentrated** はどういう意味か？

[65] **Q. terrestrial** [təréstriəl] **creatures** = animals that live on the (　　　)

[66] **scavenge:** 13 ページ注 [35] 参照。

[66] **Q. forest canopy** はどういう意味か？

[71] **terrain** [teréin, tə-] = a particular type of land

[72] **Q. furtive viewing of others** = seeing others without being (　　　)

[73] **settlement:** 定住

[73] **ensue** = happen after or as a result of another event

If the environment is deemed safe for further exploration, then other features highlight the most attractive sites. The topography must allow us to navigate easily; landmarks, bends, and variations are welcome to the eye, so long as they do not create confusing complexities, or mask dangers. We recognize, also, the encouragement to exploration that is created by the mysterious element in the terrain: the path that leads out of sight or behind a hill. Its further exploration will be safe only if it combines adventure with automatic caution and an instinct to recoil from danger. This surprising fascination with risk and danger attracts us to all manner of cultural embellishments: from horror stories and roller-coaster rides to paintings of shipwrecks and disaster movies; it springs from an inherited urge to explore and understand environments as fully as possible from the safest possible vantage-point. The fact that these hazards are potentially fatal is the reason why a desire to inform oneself more fully about their nature has selective advantage over an attitude of apathetic indifference.

There is a clear adaptive advantage to be gained by choosing environments that offer places of security and clear unimpeded views of the terrain—which allow one to see without being seen—tempered by a mysterious invitation to explore. These combinations remain an innate preference: their attractiveness informs many of our aesthetic preferences, from landscape architecture to painting. Extensive views and cosy inglenooks; daunting castles; the tree-house, the 'Little House on the Prairie'; the mysterious door in the wall of the secret garden: so many of the classically seductive landscape scenes combine symbols of refuge and safety, with the prospect of uninterrupted panoramic views; or the enticement to explore, tempered by verdant pastures and water.

[74] **deemed** = thought to be

[75] **topography:** 地形、地勢

[78] Q. **mask dangers** の意味はどれか？
1. 危険があることをわからなくする
2. 危険を和らげる
3. 危険を暗示する

[84] **all manner of . . .** = all kinds of . . .（manner が単数であることに注意）

[84] **cultural embellishments:** 文化を彩るもの。
Cf. to embellish = to beautify.

[86] Q. **disaster movies** の意味はどちらか？
1. 見るに堪えないひどい映画　2. 大災害を扱った映画

[88] **vantage-point** = a place or position affording a good view of something

[88] Q. **are potentially fatal** = (　　　) be fatal

[90] **selective advantage:** 自然選択によって生き残るために有利な特徴。
Cf. adaptive advantage（l. 92）.

[91] Q. **apathetic indifference** の対立概念を同じ段落から指摘しなさい。

[93] Q. **unimpeded** と同じ意味の単語をこの段落中から抜き出しなさい。

[95] **tempered by . . .** = combined with and made sharper by . . .
temper とは、「他のものを混ぜることによって、より望ましい状態にする」という意味。80 ページ 62 行目を参照のこと。

[97] **informs** = permeates, feeds. 目的語は many of our aesthetic preferences であり、inform A of B の形にはなっていない。

[98] **inglenooks** [íŋglnùks]: 炉端

[99] **the 'Little House on the Prairie':**『大草原の小さな家』は、ローラ・インガルス・ワイルダー（Laura Ingalls Wilder, 1867–1957）の自伝的小説シリーズ『インガルス一家の物語』の第 3 話。テレビドラマにもなった。

[100] **the mysterious door in the wall of the secret garden:** フランシス・バーネットの小説『秘密の花園』（1909）や、H・G・ウェルズの短編 *The Door in the Wall*（1911）などへの言及。

[103] **enticement** ⇐ entice（v.）誘惑する

[103] **verdant** = green with vegetation

10

The Secret Garden

(Part 2)

John D. Barrow

The combination of refuge and safety, on the one hand, and panoramic views, on the other, figures prominently in our best-appreciated landscape gardening, public parks, and gardens, where they are calculated to aid relaxation and induce feelings of ease and well-being. Distinguished architects, like Frank Lloyd Wright, have laid particular emphasis upon the desirability of creating canopies and refuges within buildings, and often set them in opposition to panoramic vistas, or even cascades of water, in order to heighten the feeling of security that these cosy alcoves create. Sloping ceilings, overhangs, gabling, and porches are all architectural features that accentuate the feeling of refuge from the outside world, while balconies, bays, and picture windows meet our desire for a wide-ranging prospect. The skilful use of trees and water in the design of buildings and gardens can reinforce these features.

On the other hand, their denial in many urban building projects has had consequences that are all too plain to see. Concrete, exposed walkways, innumerable blind corners, greyness, and banal predictability, which offer no refuge from everyone else, and buildings that offer no enticement to enter: these abominations have led to depression, crime, and emotional disequilibrium. Mike Harding's short guide to modern architecture rekindles those fears that the Psalmist had so blissfully dispelled:

[2] **Q. our best-appreciated landscape gardening . . .** = the landscape gardening . . . that (　　　) (　　　) (　　　)

[3] **landscape gardening:** 造園術、庭造り

[5] **Frank Lloyd Wright:** フランク・ロイド・ライト（1869–1959）。アメリカの建築家。東京の帝国ホテルの設計者としても有名な建築界の巨匠。

[8] **cascades of water:** 右の写真を参照のこと。cascade は階段状に連続する小さな滝（waterfall）を指し、断崖からの瀑布は cataract という。

[9] **Q. these cosy alcoves** [ǽlkouvz] は同じ文のどの部分を指しているか？

[10] **overhangs:** 屋根やバルコニーなどの張り出し

[10] **gabling** ⇐ gable（v.）: 切妻造りにする。cf. gable（n.）破風。右の図参照。

[12] **bays** = bay windows 張り出し窓

[12] **picture window:** ピクチャーウインドー（1 枚ガラスのはめ殺し窓）

[13] **Q. a wide-ranging prospect** と同じ意味の語句を同じ段落から選びなさい。

[16] **Q. their denial** はどういう意味か？

[18] **blind corners:** 見通しのきかない曲がり角

[19] **banal** [bənɑ́ːl | -nǽl]: 陳腐な、平凡な

[20] **abomination** = a thing that causes disgust and hatred. Cf. abominable = disgusting.

[21] **Q. emotional disequilibrium** [disìːkwəlíbriəm] とは何を意味するか？

[22] **Mike Harding:** マイク・ハーディング（1944–）。イギリスのシンガーソングライター、コメディアン、テレビタレント。詩人、文筆家でもある。

[23] **those fears that the Psalmist** [sɑ́ːmist] **had so blissfully dispelled:** Harding の詩が旧約聖書の『詩編』第 23 番の賛美歌のパロディであることへの言及。Psalmist は『詩編』の作者（イスラエルのダビデ王とされている）のこと。もとの詩は注 [31] を参照。

Fallingwater
or Kaufmann Residence in south-western Pennsylvania, designed by Frank Lloyd Wright in 1935

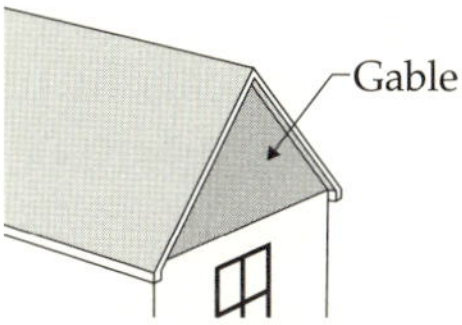

Gable

A typical contemporary urban architecture
(the epitome of banal predictability)

The planner is my shepherd:
He maketh me to walk; through dark tunnels
and underpasses he forces me to go.
He maketh concrete canyons tower above me.
By the rivers of traffic he maketh me walk.
He knocketh down all that is good, he maketh straight the
curves.
He maketh of the city a wasteland and a car park.

Our aesthetic preferences are a fusion of instinct and experience. We would expect that, in the absence of experience and special influence, our innate sensitivities for these life-supporting features of natural scenes would remain. Indeed, simple landscapes and still-life scenes are usually preferred by those with no special interest in art. A taste for the avant-garde or the abstract is a fruit of experience overriding instinct. Even then, what appeals in man-made art is the symbolic play, or counterplay, on those same adaptive features that have for so long informed traditional artistic images.

Our alertness and sensitivity to so many of the transient features of our environment—the lengthening shadows that signal the end of daylight; the darkening clouds or rushing winds that herald cold or storm; the distant horizon that hides the unknown 'over the hills and far away'—all are pointers that once rewarded response and appreciation. Shadow reveals new information about distance and depth; it offers the prospect of more detailed appraisal of the environment. Danger lurks in the shadows; it pays to be especially sensitive to it. Alertness to the sunset and the shadows that signal the coming of darkness, and the need to change patterns of behaviour in order to ensure warmth and safety, has clear advantage over disinterest.

With the darkness comes the importance of fire; flickering flames still fascinate us. The fire was the focus of life after dark, offering warmth and safety, fellowship and light. It inflames strong emotions—positive and negative—by its paradoxical offerings of comfort and danger. This odd mixture of fear and fascination appears elsewhere. Large animals are strangely attrac-

[24] **The planner:** ここでは「建築家」のこと。

[25] **He maketh me to walk** = He makes me walk（1611年刊行の『欽定訳聖書』などに出てくる古い語法。）

[25] **through dark tunnels and underpasses:** 26行目のgoを修飾する副詞句。underpassは地下道やガード下。

[27] **tower:** 動詞で、「そびえる」の意味。

[29] **he maketh straight the curves** = he makes the curves straight

[31] **He maketh of the city a wasteland and a car park:** 彼は街を荒野に、駐車場にしてしまう。目的語はa wasteland and a car park。

『詩編』23編は以下のとおり。

The LORD is my shepherd, I shall not want.	主は私の羊飼い。私は乏しいことがない。
He makes me lie down in green pastures;	主は私を緑の野に伏させ
he leads me beside still waters;	憩いの汀に伴われる。
he restores my soul.	主は私の魂を生き返らせ
He leads me in right paths	御名にふさわしく、
for His name's sake.	正しい道へと導かれる。
Even though I walk through the darkest valley,	たとえ死の陰の谷を歩むとも
I fear no evil;	私は災いを恐れない。
for you are with me;	あなたは私と共におられ
your rod and your staff—	あなたの鞭と杖が
they comfort me.	私を慰める。
You prepare a table before me	私を苦しめる者の前で
in the presence of my enemies;	あなたは私に食卓を整えられる。
you anoint my head with oil;	私の頭に油を注ぎ
my cup overflows.	私の杯を満たされる。
Surely goodness and mercy shall follow me	命あるかぎり
all the days of my life,	恵みと慈しみが私を追う。
and I shall dwell in the house of the LORD	私は主の家に住もう
my whole life long.	日の続くかぎり。

（日本聖書協会「賛歌　ダビデの詩」『聖書　聖書協会共同訳』）

[36] **still-life:**（絵画や写真の題材としての）静物

[39] **the symbolic play, or counterplay, on . . . :** play onはinventive use ofの意味。counterplay on...は、～をわざと外した表現をするという意味。

[41] **informed:** 75ページ注[97]参照。

[42] **transient** [trǽnziənt | -ʃənt] = fleeting, temporary

[46] **'over the hills and far away':**「丘を越えてはるか彼方へ」。17世紀イギリスの民謡でよく用いられたフレーズ。

[47] **rewarded response and appreciation** = rewarded us with information which helped us to survive if we responded to them and appreciated them

[50] **Q. it pays** はどういう意味か？

[57] **Q.** positive emotion, negative emotion の例を英語で挙げなさい。

tive, yet threatening. Large animals were once both a danger and a ready source of abundant food. Our instinctive attraction to them, tempered by fear and respect, looks like a remnant of a reaction that increased the likelihood of survival, as compared with a response of total fear and isolation, or one of reckless familiarity. Animals were the key to our ancestors' survival. It is not surprising that instinctive reactions to them evolved and spread. The instinctiveness of those reactions explains the propensity we have for symbolism that uses animals. The dominance of the lion, the soaring freedom of the eagle, the evil serpent, the fleetness of the gazelle—these are some of the symbols that trade upon our environmental history.

For tropical savannah-dwellers, daily changes in light and temperature are regular and rapid, but other critical changes are slow and subtle. We would therefore expect to find adaptations in humans that display sensitivities to indicators of seasonal change and of imminent rainfall and fruitfulness. We find emotional responses to the seasonal changes in the colours of leaves and shrubs: people flock to New Hampshire for the fall. We find flowers beautiful, therapeutic, and romantic. What hospital ward would be without them? What more frequent gift for a loved one? What more common still-life subject? Our unusual interest in colourful flowers and the lengths to which we go to cultivate and arrange them are impressive. We don't eat flowers, but the appearance of flowers is a useful cue that allows different plant forms to be rapidly identified and distinguished. If no flowers are present, then plants are all green, and can be distinguished only by detailed inspection. Flowers also give information about the ripeness of fruit. Thus, while plants burst into flower for reasons that have nothing to do with our likes or dislikes, the fact that a sensitivity to flowers has a purpose, which is adaptive, provides us with a clue to the origin of what would otherwise be an entirely mysterious fascination.

It has become fashionable to regard human aesthetic preferences as entirely subjective responses to learning and nurture. This now seems barely credible. Our sensitivities and emotional responses have not been created out of nothing. The evaluation

[61] Q. **Our instinctive attraction to them** = The fact that we are (　　　) (　　　) (　　　) (　　　).

[62] **temper:** 75 ページ注 [95] 参照。

[62] **remnant** = a small remaining part

[63] **as compared with . . . :** ～とは対照的に。同じような表現として、A as distinct from B、A as in contrast with B などがあるが、いずれも B という対立概念を示すことによって A という概念の意味をはっきりさせようとする表現。例えば、水の液体としての側面を強調したければ water as compared with ice と表現したり、水の粘性のない特徴を強調したければ、water as compared with oil と表現できる。

[64] Q. **reckless familiarity** の意味はどれか？

1. 思慮を欠く油断
2. 分け隔てない親しみ
3. 無思慮ななれなれしさ

[67] **propensity for . . . :** ～への傾向、好み

[69] **soar** [sɔː(r)] = fly up

[71] **trade upon . . .** = take advantage of . . .

[73] Q. **critical changes** の critical はどういう意味か？

1. 危機的な　　2. 境界的な　　3. きわめて重要な

[76] **imminent** = likely to happen very soon

[78] **New Hampshire:** ニューハンプシャー。アメリカ北東部の州。特に、バーモント州と接している地域は紅葉が美しいことで有名。

[79] **therapeutic** [θèrəpjúːtik] ⇐ therapy

[79] Q. **What hospital ward would be without them?:** どんな病棟（hospital ward）にも何があるはずだと言っているのか？

[81] Q. **What more common still-life subject** than (　　　)?

[82] **the lengths to which we go . . . :** go to all length(s) または go to great length(s)（どんな苦労もいとわない、徹底的にやる）という表現が基になっている。

[91] Q. **what would otherwise be an entirely mysterious fascination** = our fascination with (　　　), which would be entirely mysterious (　　　) we did not know that a sensitivity to flowers has a purpose . . .

[94] Q. **learning and nurture** の反対概念は何か？ 同じ段落から 1 語を選びなさい。

of environments was a crucial instinct for our distant ancestors, one upon which their very survival depended.

One should also appreciate that these ideas about the origins of aesthetic response would be regarded as deeply heretical by many art critics, who like to believe that artistic appreciation is immune from 'scientific' analysis. But consider how we have long appreciated the role of mathematical structures in aesthetics. We use particular shapes or symmetrical patterns when we wish to emphasize these underlying mathematical harmonies. Our knowledge of the behaviour of light, or the perception of colour, which was made possible by the studies of physicists, is exploited to the full to create images that are attractive and pleasing to the eye. One might suspect that our affinity for these geometrical and optical patterns is linked to the ease with which the brain can produce mental models of them, and the extent to which they are instantiated into the natural world in situations where their recognition will be rewarded. These important mathematical and optical aspects of aesthetics must be added to the biological perspective that adaptive evolution provides.

[98] Q. **one** = an (　　　)

[99] Q. **appreciate** の意味はどれか？

1. 賞賛する　2. 鑑賞する　3. 正しく認識する

[100] **heretical** ⇐ heretic 異端者

[106] **behaviour of light:** behaviour は、特定の状態のもとで物体・物質の示す性質という意味。

[110] Q. **geometrical and optical patterns** とは何か？

[112] Q. **they are instantiated into the natural world** の意味はどれか？

1. それらが自然界に実現されている
2. それらが自然の中に例示されている
3. それらの例が自然の中に導入されている

[113] **where their recognition will be rewarded:** their は 110 行目の geometrical and optical patterns を指す。

[115] Q. **perspective** の意味はどれか？

1. 視点　2. 眺望　3. 透視図

A cave painting of aurochs at Lascaux, France, thought to be about 17,300 years old

11

Heroic Contrasts: The Extraordinary versus the Banal

(Part 1)

Philip G. Zimbardo

The solitary heroic figure, like the brave marshal in a western movie who faces down a band of renegades, is supported, more often than not, by groups of people working in unison in emergencies, disasters, and situations that demand concerted action. The Underground Railroad, which took southern slaves to freedom in northern towns, could function only with the coordinated efforts of many people who worked in peril of their lives. Similarly, first responders to disasters are typically citizen volunteers working in loosely organized teams. Many individuals working in collective harmony are anonymous. They brave danger without expectation of personal reward but for the sake of answering a call to community service.

To the traditionally accepted notion that heroes are exceptional people, we can therefore add an opposing perspective—that some heroes are ordinary people who have done something extraordinary. The first image is the more romantic and is favored in ancient myth and modern media. It suggests that the hero has done something that ordinary people in the same position would not or could not have done. These superstars must have been born with a hero gene. They are the exception to the rule.

Our second perspective, however, directs us to examine the interaction between situation and person, the dynamic that impelled an individual to act heroically at a particular time and

[About the Author]

Philip G. Zimbardo: フィリップ・ジョージ・ジンバルドー（1933–）。アメリカの社会心理学者。スタンフォード大学教授。代表的著作に『現代心理学』古畑和孝・平井久訳、全3巻（サイエンス社、1981–83）がある。本章は、*The Lucifer Effect: Understanding How Good People Turn Evil*（New York: Random House, 2008）からの一節。

[1] **marshal:**（西部劇の）保安官

[2] Q. **faces down** の意味はどれか？
1. 顔を伏せる　2. 面目をつぶす　3. 勇敢に立ち向かう

[2] **renegades** [rénigèidz]**:** 裏切り者、変節漢

[2] **more often than not:** たいてい（= as often as not）

[4] Q. **concerted** [kənsə́ːrtid] **action** はどういう意味か？

[5] **The Underground Railroad:** 19世紀アメリカ南部の黒人奴隷が、奴隷制が認められていた南部から、奴隷制が廃止されていた北部の州やカナダへ自由を求めて逃れるために利用した秘密のルートや隠れ家、またその地下組織。秘密結社「地下鉄道」と呼ばれたのは、奴隷たちを誘導する係を「車掌」、隠れ家を「駅」、逃亡中の奴隷を「乗客」などとする隠語を用いたため。

Harriet Tubman
A key figure in the Underground Railroad

[6] Q. **coordinated efforts** はどういう意味か？

[10] Q. **in collective harmony** = in harmony as a (　　)

[10] Q. **brave** の意味はどれか？
1. 英雄　2. 勇ましい　3. ～をものともしない

[12] Q. **call** の意味はどれか？
1. 電話　2. 叫び声　3. 呼びかけ

[24] Q. **at a particular time and place** の意味はどちらか？
1. ある特殊な時と場所で　2. ある時、ある場所で

place. A situation may act either as a catalyst, encouraging action, or it may reduce barriers to action, such as the formation of a collective social support network. It is remarkable that in most instances people who have engaged in heroic action repeatedly reject the name of hero.

Such doers of heroic deeds typically argue that they were simply taking an action that seemed necessary at the time. They are convinced that anybody would have acted similarly, or else they find it difficult to understand why others did not. Nelson Mandela has said, 'I was not a messiah, but an ordinary man who had become a leader because of extraordinary circumstances.' Phrases like this are used by people at all levels of society who have acted heroically: 'It was nothing special'; 'I did what had to be done.' These are the refrains of the 'ordinary' or everyday warrior, our 'banal hero.' Let's contrast such positive banality with what Hannah Arendt has taught us to call 'the banality of evil.'

On the Banality of Evil

This concept emerged from Arendt's observations at the trial of Adolf Eichmann, indicted for crimes against humanity because he helped to orchestrate the genocide of European Jews. In *Eichmann in Jerusalem: A Report on the Banality of Evil,* Arendt formulates the idea that such individuals should not be viewed as exceptions, as monsters, or as perverted sadists. She argues that such dispositional attributes, typically applied to perpetrators of evil deeds, serve to set them apart from the rest of the human community. Instead, Eichmann and others like him, Arendt says, should be exposed in their very ordinariness. When we realize this, we become more aware that such people are a pervasive, hidden danger in all societies. Eichmann's defense was that he was simply following orders. Of this mass murderer's motives and conscience, Arendt notes:

> As for his base motives, he was perfectly sure that he was not what he called an *innerer Schweinehund,* a dirty

[25] Q. **catalyst:** なぜ catalyst（触媒）と言えるのか説明しなさい。

[33] **Nelson Mandela:** ネルソン・マンデラ（1918–2013）。南アフリカ共和国の政治指導者で、反アパルトヘイト運動家として活躍し 1964 年に投獄されたが、1990 年に解放され、大統領となった。

[34] **messiah** [misáiə, mə-, mɛ-]**:** 救世主

[39] Q. **banal** はどういう意味か？

1. not special　2. very familiar

[40] Q. **positive** はどういう意味か？

1. 間違いのない　2. 実証的な　3. 好ましい

[40] **Hannah Arendt:** ハンナ（ハナ）・アーレント（1906–75）。ドイツ生まれのアメリカの政治思想家。全体主義を生み出した現代社会の病理を探究した *The Origins of Totalitarianism*『全体主義の起源』（1951）や、政治とは何かを問うた *The Human Condition*『人間の条件』（1958）が有名。

Hannah Arendt

[44] **Adolf Eichmann:** アドルフ・アイヒマン（1906–62）。ナチスドイツの親衛隊将校で、ユダヤ人の大量殺戮、いわゆる「ホロコースト」の責任者の一人。第二次世界大戦の終了後は偽名のもとにアルゼンチンで暮らしていたが、1960 年にイスラエルに連行され、裁判を受けて有罪となり、1962 年に処刑された。

Adolf Eichmann

[44] **indicted** [indáitid] ⇐ indict someone for . . . ～で人を起訴する

[44] Q. **crimes against humanity** はどういう意味か？

1. 人類を陥れる罪　2. 人道に対する犯罪

[45] Q. **orchestrate** はどういう意味か？

[46] ***Eichmann in Jerusalem: A Report on the Banality of Evil:***『イェルサレムのアイヒマン』。ハンナ・アーレントによるアイヒマンの裁判記録。1963 年に雑誌 *New Yorker* に連載された。

[49] **dispositional**（⇐ disposition）**:** 気質上の

[50] Q. **set them apart from the rest of the human community** = treat them as essentially (　　　) from other humans

[52] Q. **exposed in their very ordinariness** = examined and shown as an absolutely (　　　) human being, not as a monster

[55] Q. **mass murderer** はどういう意味か？

[58] ***innerer Schweinehund:***【ドイツ語】紳士然と振る舞っているが、心の中では極悪非道なことを考えている者。

> bastard in the depths of his heart; and as for his conscience, he remembered perfectly well that he would have had a bad conscience only if he had not done what he had been ordered to do—to ship millions of men, women, and children to their death with great zeal and the most meticulous care.

What is most striking in Arendt's account of Eichmann is all the ways in which he seemed absolutely normal and totally ordinary:

> Half a dozen psychiatrists had certified him as 'normal'—'More normal, at any rate, than I am after having examined him,' one of them was said to have exclaimed, while another had found that his whole psychological outlook, his attitude toward his wife and children, mother and father, brothers, sisters, and friends was 'not only normal but most desirable.'

Arendt's now-classic conclusion:

> The trouble with Eichmann was precisely that so many were like him, and that the many were neither perverted nor sadistic, that they were, and still are, terribly and terrifyingly normal. From the viewpoint of our legal institutions and our moral standards of judgment, this normality was much more terrifying than all the atrocities put together, for it implied . . . that this new type of criminal . . . commits his crimes under circumstances that make it well-nigh impossible for him to know or feel that he is doing wrong.

Then came her punch line, describing Eichmann's dignified march to the gallows:

> It was as though in those last minutes he was summing up the lesson that this long course in human wickedness had taught us—the lesson of the fearsome, word-and-thought-defying banality of evil.

[60] Q. **have a bad conscience** の意味はどれか？
1. 良心が痛む　2. 善悪判断ができない　3. 意識がはっきりしない

[62] **to ship** = to send

[65] **all the ways in which he seemed absolutely normal . . .** = that he seemed absolutely normal . . . in every way

[68] **psychiatrists** [sikáiətrists, sai-]**:** 精神科医

[69] Q. **'More normal, at any rate, than I am after having examined him'** suggests that the psychiatrist who examined him could not stay (　　) because she or he was shocked to find him (　　).

[71] Q. **psychological outlook** の意味はどちらか？
1. 精神構造　2. 心理学的な見通し

[75] Q. **classic** の意味はどれか？
1. 典型的な　2. 由緒正しい　3. 広く一流と認められている

[78] Q. **terrifyingly normal** = so normal that it is (　　)

[83] **well-nigh** [wɛ́lnáɪ, we-] = almost

[86] Q. **punch line** はどういう意味か？

[87] **march to the gallows:** 絞首台への行進。皮肉のこもった表現。gallows（絞首台）は単数でも s をつけて用いる。ベルリオーズ『幻想交響曲』第4楽章（'March to the Gallows'）を意識した表現であろう。

[89] Q. **lesson** の意味はどれか？
1. 教訓　2. 見本　3. 教科

[89] Q. **course** の意味はどれか？
1. 人生　2. 過程　3. 授業

[90] Q. **word-and-thought-defying banality of evil** = banality of evil that (　　) the word and thought.　さらに言い換えれば、banality of evil that is hard to think about or put into words.

The notion that 'ordinary men' can commit atrocities has been more fully developed by the historian Christopher Browning. He uncovered the systematic and personal annihilation of Jews in remote Polish villages that was committed by hundreds of men in Reserve Police Battalion 101, sent to Poland from Hamburg, Germany. These middle-aged, family men of working-class and lower-middle-class backgrounds shot thousands of unarmed Jews—men, women, the elderly, and children—and arranged for the deportation to death camps of thousands more. Yet Browning contends in his book that they were all 'ordinary men.' He believes that the mass-murder policies of the Nazi regime 'were not aberrational or exceptional events . . . As the story of Reserve Battalion 101 demonstrates, mass murder and routine had become one. Normality itself had become exceedingly abnormal.'

The psychologist Ervin Staub holds a similar view. His extensive research led him to the conclusion that 'Evil that arises out of ordinary thinking and is committed by ordinary people is the norm, not the exception.' Cruelty should be attributed to its social origins more than to its 'characterological' determinants or 'faulty personalities,' according to Zygmunt Bauman's analysis of the horrors of the Holocaust. Bauman believes further that the exception to this norm is the rare individual who has the capacity to assert moral autonomy in resisting the demands

Adolf Eichmann at his trial in Jerusalem in 1961 for crimes against humanity, war crimes, and crimes against the Jewish people

[93] **Christopher Browning:** クリストファー・ブラウニング（1944–）。アメリカの歴史家。ホロコーストの研究家。代表的著作に *Ordinary Men: Reserve Police Battalion 101 and the Final Solution in Poland*（1992）。現在イギリスのウォリック大学教授。

[94] Q. **systematic and personal:** この場合の systematic と personal は、それぞれどういう意味か？

[94] **annihilation** [ənàiəléiʃən]**:** 絶滅、掃滅

[95] **Polish:** ポーランドの

[96] **Reserve Police Battalion 101:** 第101警察予備大隊。Reserve は正規軍ではなく、警察予備官たちの部隊であることを意味する。

[96] **Hamburg:** ハンブルク。ドイツ北部の港市。

[97] **working-class:** 労働者階級の

[98] **lower-middle-class:** 中産階級の下流

[99] Q. **arranged for the deportation to death camps of thousands more** = arranged to send additional thousands of（　　　）people to death camps

[102] **regime** [rəʒíːm, rei-]**:** 支配体制、政権

[103] **aberrational** [æ̀bəréiʃənəl] ⇐ aberration 常軌を外れること

[104] Q. **routine** の意味はどちらか？
1. 日常の仕事　　2. お決まりの方法、常套手段

[106] **Ervin Staub:** アーヴィン・ストーブ（1938–）。ハンガリー、ブダペスト生まれ。アメリカのマサチューセッツ大学名誉教授。社会心理学が専門。

[110] **characterological** ⇐ characterology 性格学

[110] **determinants:** factors which decisively affect the nature or outcome of something

[111] **Zygmunt Bauman:** ジグムント・バウマン（1925–）。ポーランドの社会学者。1971年、反ユダヤ主義の運動によってポーランドを追われ、イギリスに渡り、リーズ大学で教鞭をとった。現在は同大学の名誉教授。近代とホロコーストなどについて著作が多数あり、邦訳も多い。

[112] **Holocaust:** 普通名詞としては「大量虐殺」という意味だが、頭文字を大文字で記した場合は、第2次世界大戦中にナチによって行われたヨーロッパのユダヤ人大虐殺を意味する。

[114] Q. **moral autonomy** はどういう意味か？

of destructive authorities. Such a person is rarely aware that he or she possesses this hidden strength until put to the test.

From her in-depth analysis of soldiers trained by the Greek military junta to be state-sanctioned torturers (1967–1974), my colleague the Greek psychologist Mika Haritos-Fatouros concluded that torturers are not born but made by their training. 'Anybody's son will do' is her answer to the question 'Who will make an effective torturer?' In a matter of a few months, ordinary young men from rural villages became 'weaponized' by their training in cruelty to act like brute beasts capable of inflicting the most horrendous acts of humiliation, pain, and suffering on anyone labeled 'the enemy,' who, of course, were all citizens of their own country. Such conclusions are not limited to one nation, but are common in many totalitarian regimes. We studied 'violence workers' in Brazil, policemen who tortured and murdered other Brazilian citizens for the ruling military junta. They too were 'ordinary men,' based on all the evidence we could amass.

The corpses of 22 of the Jewish women whom the Germans killed in Helmbrechts

[116] **until put to the test** = until a crisis occurs

[117] **in-depth** = detailed

[118] **junta** [húntə, dʒʌ́n-]: 軍事政権。1967年から1974年まで、ギリシャは軍事政権が支配していた。ギリシャの現代史については、テオ・アンゲロプロス（1935–2012）の映画『旅芸人の記録』（1975）などを参照。

[118] Q. **state-sanctioned torturers**（= torturers sanctioned by the state）はどういう意味か？

[122] **make** = become

[122] **In a matter of** = In no more than about

[123] Q. **'weaponized'**「武器化する」とは、誰が誰の武器となるのか？

[125] **horrendous** = extremely shocking

[128] **totalitarian:** 全体主義（totalitarianism）の、一党独裁主義の

12

Heroic Contrasts: The Extraordinary versus the Banal
(Part 2)

Philip G. Zimbardo

On the Banality of Heroism

The banality of evil shares much with the banality of heroism. Neither attribute is the direct consequence of unique dispositional tendencies; there are no special inner attributes of either pathology or goodness residing within the human psyche or the human genome. Both conditions emerge in particular situations at particular times when situational forces play a compelling role in moving particular individuals across a decisional line from inaction to action. There is a decisive decisional moment when a person is caught up in a vector of forces that emanate from a behavioral context. Those forces combine to increase the probability of one's acting to harm others or acting to help others. Their decision may or may not be consciously planned or mindfully taken. Rather, strong situational forces most often impulsively drive the person to action. Among the situational action vectors are: group pressures and group identity, the diffusion of responsibility for the action, a temporal focus on the immediate moment without concern for consequences stemming from the act in the future, presence of social models, and commitment to an ideology.

A common theme in the accounts of European Christians who helped the Jews during the Holocaust could be summed up as the 'banality of goodness.' What is striking over and over again

[3] Q. **Neither attribute** = Neither (　　　) nor (　　　)

[3] Q. **unique dispositional tendencies** はどういう意味か？
1. 独特な気質の諸傾向　2. 性格面でのユニークな傾向
3. 普通の人間にはない特異な人格

[5] Q. **pathology** の意味はどれか？　1. 病状　2. 病理学　3. 病的逸脱

[5] **psyche** [sáiki]: 心（発音に注意）

[6] **genome** [dʒíːnoum]: ゲノム。ここでは「ある生物のすべての遺伝情報」の意味で用いられている。本来の定義では、生物が生きていくのに最小限必要な染色体の1組。

[8] Q. **decisional** の意味はどれか？
1. 決断の　2. 判決の　3. 堅忍不抜の

[10] Q. **vector of forces** はどのような意味か？

[10] **emanate from** = originate from; stem from（Cf. l. 18.）

[11] **a behavioral context:** ある行為を行う背景。79行目も参照。

[14] **mindfully** = carefully, with proper attention

[15] **Among the situational action vectors** = Some of the situational action vectors

[16] Q. **diffusion of responsibility** は何を意味しているか？

[17] Q. **temporal** の意味はどれか？　1. 一時の　2. 現世の　3. 時間の

[19] Q. **commitment to an ideology** はどういう意味か？

1955年12月アラバマ州モンゴメリーにて市営バスに乗車したローザ・パークスが白人乗客に席を譲れと運転手に命じられて拒絶して逮捕されたのを機に、社会活動家エドガー・ニクソンやキング牧師らがバス・ボイコット運動を展開。写真左は1956年2月に運動の首謀者として起訴されて、指紋をとられているところ。バス事業は財政破綻の危機に瀕し、1956年11月連邦最高裁判所はモンゴメリーの人種隔離政策に違憲判決を下して、運動は同年12月20日に公式に終了した。写真右は12月21日に市営バスに乗るローザ・パークス。次ページ30行目以降を参照のこと。

is the number of these rescuers who did the right thing without considering themselves heroic, who acted merely out of a sense of common decency. The ordinariness of their goodness is especially striking in the context of the incredible evil of the systematic genocide by Nazis on a scale the world had never before experienced.

The heroic action of Rosa Parks's refusal to sit in the 'colored' section in the back of an Alabama bus, of Joe Darby's exposing the Abu Ghraib tortures, or of the first responders' rush to the World Trade Center disaster are acts of bravery that occur at particular times and places. In contrast, the heroism of Mohandas Gandhi or Mother Teresa consists of valorous acts repeated over a lifetime.

This perception implies that any of us could as easily become heroes as perpetrators of evil depending on how we are influenced by situational forces. The imperative becomes discovering how to limit, constrain, and prevent the situational and systemic forces that propel some of us toward social pathology. But equally important is the injunction for every society to foster a 'heroic imagination' in its citizenry. It is achieved by conveying the message that every person is a hero in waiting who will be counted upon to do the right thing when the moment of decision comes. The decisive question for each of us is whether to act in help of others, to prevent harm to others, or not to act at all. We should be preparing many laurel wreaths for all those who will discover their reservoir of hidden strengths and virtues enabling them to come forth to act against injustice and cruelty and to stand up for their principled values.

The large body of research on situational determinants of antisocial behavior, and particularly Milgram's famous work, reveals the extent to which normal, ordinary people can be led to engage in cruel acts against innocent others. However, in those studies and many others, while the majority obeyed, conformed, complied, were persuaded, and were seduced, there was always a minority who resisted, dissented, and disobeyed. In one sense, heroism lies in the ability to resist powerful situational forces that so readily entrap most people.

[25] **Q. out of a sense of common decency** はどういう意味か？

1. 一般の人々への親切心から
2. 人間に共通する礼儀感覚から
3. ごく普通の人間として当たり前のことだと思って

[27] **Q. systematic genocide** はどういう意味か？

[30] **Rosa Parks:** ローザ・パークス（1913–2005）。アメリカの公民権運動の活動家。95ページのコラム参照のこと。

[30] **Q. 'colored' section** はどういう意味か？

[31] **Joe Darby:** ジョー（ジョーゼフ）・ダービー。ダービーは、2004年1月、イラクのアブグレイブ刑務所（Abu Ghraib prison）に収容されたイラク人兵士に対し、この施設を監督していた米軍関係者が非人道的な扱いをし、拷問を加えている写真をマスコミに公表した。

[32] **the first responders** = those who reacted instantly to the disaster

[32] **the World Trade Center disaster:** ニューヨークの世界貿易センタービルにイスラム過激派のハイジャックした旅客機が突入した、2001年9月11日の「同時多発テロ事件」への言及。

[34] **Mohandas Gandhi:** モハンダス・ガンジー（1869–1948）。インドの政治指導者・民族主義者。非暴力的抵抗を貫いたインド建国の父。

[35] **Mother Teresa:** マザー・テレサ（1910–97）。ユーゴスラビア生まれの修道女。カルカッタで貧民救済に献身し、1979年にノーベル平和賞を受賞。

[35] **valorous** [vǽlərəs] = brave

[39] **Q. The imperative becomes discovering . . .** = It becomes absolutely (　　　) to discover . . .

[40] **Q. constrain** の意味はどれか？

1. 束縛する　　2. 強制する　　3. 封じ込める

[41] **propel** = urge

[44] **a hero in waiting:** 機会がめぐってきたら、その本性を発揮するが、今はそれと認められていない英雄。91行目も参照。

[45] **counted upon** = relied upon

[48] **Q. laurel wreaths** [ríːθs, ríːðz] の（a）文字どおりの意味と、この場合の（b）比喩的な意味は何か？

[49] **reservoir** [rézəvwàː | rézərvwàːr, -vɔ̀ːr]**:** 蓄え

[51] **principled values** = values morally desirable and consistent

[53] **Milgram:** スタンリー・ミルグラム（1933–84）。アメリカの社会心理学者。閉鎖的な状況のもとで、権威者の指示に従う人間心理を研究するために、いわゆる Milgram experiment（ミルグラム実験）を行ったことで有名。

Are the personalities of the resisters different from those of the blindly obedient? Are they like Clark Kent, whose normal appearance conceals Superman's extraordinary powers? Not at all. Rather, our banality of heroism conception maintains that doers of heroic deeds of the moment are not essentially different from those who comprise the base rate of the easily seduced. There is not much empirical research on which to base such assertions. Because heroism is not a simple phenomenon that can be studied systematically, it defies clean definitions and on-the-spot data collection. Heroic acts are ephemeral and unpredictable, and appreciation of them is decidedly retrospective. Because heroes are usually interviewed months or years after their heroic behavior has occurred, we generally do not know what the decision matrix for heroes is at the time they elect to engage in risk-laden activities.

What seems evident is that heroic behavior is rare enough not to be readily predictable by any psychological assessments of personality. They measure individual differences between people in their usual, standard behavioral settings, not in the atypical settings that often elicit heroic deeds.

For reasons we do not yet fully understand, thousands of ordinary people in every country around the world, when they are placed in special circumstances, make the decision to act heroically. On the face of it, the perspective we take here seems to deflate the myth of the hero and to make something special into something banal. This is not so, however, because our position still recognizes that the act of heroism is indeed special and rare. Heroism supports the ideals of a community and serves as an extraordinary guide, and it provides an exemplary role model for prosocial behavior. The banality of heroism means that we are all heroes in waiting. It is a choice that we may all be called upon to make at some point in time. I believe that by making heroism an egalitarian attribute of human nature rather than a rare feature of the elect few, we can better foster heroic acts in every community. According to journalist Carol Depino 'Everyone has the capability of becoming a hero in one degree or another. Sometimes you might not realize it. To someone it

[62] **Q. the blindly obedient** = people who (　　　) blindly

[63] **Superman:** スーパーマン。1938年に登場したアメリカの漫画のヒーロー。後にテレビ化、映画化された。スーパーマンは普段は新聞記者クラーク・ケント (Clark Kent) として暮らしていたが、最近は新聞社を辞めたという説もある。

[64] **Q. maintains** の意味はどちらか？
1. 維持する　　2. 主張する

[66] **comprise** = be composed of; consist of. Cf. l. 35.

[66] **base rate:** 平均基準

[66] **Q. the easily seduced** はどういう意味か？

[67] **Q. empirical research** の意味はどちらか？
1. 実証的研究　　2. 観察のみに頼った調査

[69] **Q. defies clean definitions** はどういう意味か？

[70] **Q.** on-the-spot は「現場での」という意味。では、**on-the-spot data collection** はどういう意味か？

[70] **ephemeral** [ifém(ə)rəl] = temporary; transitory; transient; fleeting

[71] **Q. appreciation of them** = recognition of (　　　) (　　　) as such

[71] **Q. retrospective** の意味はどれか？
1. 追憶的な　　2. 回想が好きな　　3. 振り返ってみてわかる

[74] **Q. decision matrix** はどういう意味か？

[75] **risk-laden:** 危険をはらんだ。~-laden は「~を積んだ、~でいっぱいの」という意味。57ページ注 [57] 参照。

[79] **behavioral settings:** ある行為を行う「場面」という意味。11行目参照。

[80] **atypical** = not typical

[84] **Q. On the face of it** はどういう意味か？

[85] **Q. deflate** の文字どおりの意味は inflate (名詞が inflation) の逆で、「(膨らんだものを) しぼませる、へこませる」という意味だが、ここではどういう意味か？

[86] **Q. our position** は具体的にどういう意味か？

[89] **Q. role model** はどういう意味か？

[90] **prosocial** (= pro + social)**:** pro- は「~のため (for)」という意味の接頭語。

[92] **called upon** = required

[92] **Q. make** の意味上の目的語は何か？

[93] **Q. an egalitarian attribute of human nature** = an attribute (　　　) to all humanity

[94] **elect:** 【神学】神によって選ばれた。Cf. l. 75.

[94] **foster** = promote the growth or development of; encourage; nurture

could be as small as holding a door open and saying "hello" to them. We are all heroes to someone.'

13

Evolved for Cancer?

(Part 1)

Carl Zimmer

Natural selection is not natural perfection. Living creatures have evolved some remarkably complex adaptations, but we are still very vulnerable to disease. Among the most tragic of those ills—and perhaps most enigmatic—is cancer. A cancerous tumor is exquisitely well adapted for survival in its own grotesque way. Its cells continue to divide long after ordinary cells would stop. They destroy surrounding tissues to make room for themselves, and they trick the body into supplying them with energy to grow even larger. But the tumors that afflict us are not foreign parasites that have acquired sophisticated strategies for attacking bodies. They are made of our own cells, turned against us. Nor is cancer some bizarre rarity: a woman in the U.S. has a 39 percent chance of being diagnosed with some type of cancer in her lifetime. A man has a 45 percent chance.

These facts make cancer a grim yet fascinating puzzle for evolutionary biologists. If natural selection is powerful enough to produce complex adaptations, from the eye to the immune system, why has it been unable to wipe out cancer? The answer, these investigators argue, lies in the evolutionary process itself. Natural selection has favored certain defenses against cancer but cannot eliminate it altogether. Ironically, natural selection may even inadvertently provide some of the tools that cancer cells can use to grow.

[About the Author]

Carl Zimmer: カール・ジマー（1966–）。イエール大学モース・カレッジの特別研究員。*The New York Times* や *Discover* などの雑誌に定期的に執筆する著述家。一般向けの科学啓蒙書を多数執筆している。邦訳書に『進化——生命のたどる道』長谷川眞理子監修訳（岩波書店、2012）、『大腸菌——進化のカギを握るミクロな生命体』矢野真千子訳（日本放送出版協会、2009）、『「進化」大全——ダーウィン思想：史上最大の科学革命』渡辺政隆訳（光文社、2004）など。本章は、Sylvia Nasar and Jesse Cohen, eds, *The Best American Science Writing 2008* (New York: HarperCollins, 2008) からの一節。

[4] **cancerous tumor:** 悪性腫瘍

[7] **tissues:**（生体の）組織。Cf. organ 器官。

[8] **trick** (someone) **into . . . ing:**（人を）騙して〜させる。27 ページ注 [117] を参照のこと。

[9] Q. **foreign** の意味はどれか？
1. 外来の　2. 適切でない　3. 見慣れない

[11] Q. **turned against us** はどういう意味か？

[13] Q. **chance** の意味はどれか？
1. 機会　2. 偶然　3. 可能性

[17] **the eye:** 眼は、伸縮するレンズなど複雑なメカニズムによって成立している器官なので、進化論では定番のように持ち出される例となっている。

[20] Q. **Natural selection has favored . . .** とはどういう意味か？ 69 ページ注 [3] を参照のこと。

[21] Q. **eliminate** と同じ意味の語（句）を同じ段落から探しなさい。

[22] Q. **inadvertently** [inədvə́ːrt(ə)ntli] に含まれない意味はどれか？
1. carelessly　2. elaborately　3. unintentionally

Session 13

The Dawn of Cancer

At its root, cancer is a disease of multicellularity. Our single-celled ancestors reproduced by dividing in two. After animals emerged, about seven hundred million years ago, the cells inside their bodies continued to reproduce by dividing, using the molecular machinery they inherited from their progenitors. The cells also began to specialize as they divided, forming different tissues. The complex, multicellular bodies animals have today were made possible by the emergence of new genes that could control how cells divided—such as by stopping the cells' reproduction once an organ reached its adult size. The millions of animal species are evidence of the great evolutionary success that came with acquiring a body. But bodies also present a profound risk. Whenever a cell inside a body divides, its DNA has a small chance of acquiring a cancer-causing mutation. "Every time a cell divides, it's going to be at risk of developing into cancer," says Judith Campisi of Lawrence Berkeley National Laboratory.

Rare mutations, for instance, may cause a cell to lose restraint and begin to multiply uncontrollably. Other mutations can add to the problem: they may allow deranged cells to invade surrounding tissues and spread through the body. Or they may allow tumor cells to evade the immune system or attract blood vessels that can supply fresh oxygen.

Cancer, in other words, re-creates within our own bodies the evolutionary process that enables animals to adapt to their environment. At the level of organisms, natural selection operates when genetic mutations cause some organisms to have more reproductive success than others; the mutations get "selected" in the sense that they persist and become more common in future generations. In cancer, cells play the role of organisms. Cancer-causing changes to DNA cause some cells to reproduce more effectively than ordinary ones. And even within a single tumor, more adapted cells may outcompete less successful ones. "It's like Darwinian evolution, except that it hap-

[25] **multicellularity** [mʌltisèljəlǽrəti] ⇐ multicellular 多細胞の

[25] **single-celled:** 単細胞の

[29] **progenitors:** (生物学的な) 先祖、(動植物の) 原種

[30] Q. **specialize** はどういう意味か？

[38] **mutation:** 突然変異

[39] **at risk of . . . :** ～の危険がある。Cf. at the risk of . . . ～の危険を冒して

[40] **Judith Campisi:** ジュディス・キャンピージ。116 ページ 105 行目に出てくる Christopher Benz と同じく、アメリカ合衆国カリフォルニア州にあるバック研究所 (Buck Institute) の教授。老化の研究を行っている。

[40] **Lawrence Berkeley National Laboratory:** ローレンス・バークリー国立研究所。アメリカ合衆国カリフォルニア州にある研究所。

[43] Q. **add to the problem** = make the situation (　　　) serious

[44] Q. **deranged cells** = cells that are (　　　) of control, behaving unpredictably

[46] **blood vessels:** 血管

[53] Q. **"selected"** はなぜ引用符で囲われているのか？

[53] Q. **persist** の意味はどれか？

1. insist　　2. survive　　3. maintain

[57] **outcompete:** (ライバルを) うち負かす。out- は動詞と結合して「～をうち負かす」という意味の他動詞を作る接頭語。Cf. outlive, outshine, outmanoeuvre など。

[58] Q. **Darwinian evolution** とはどのような概念か？

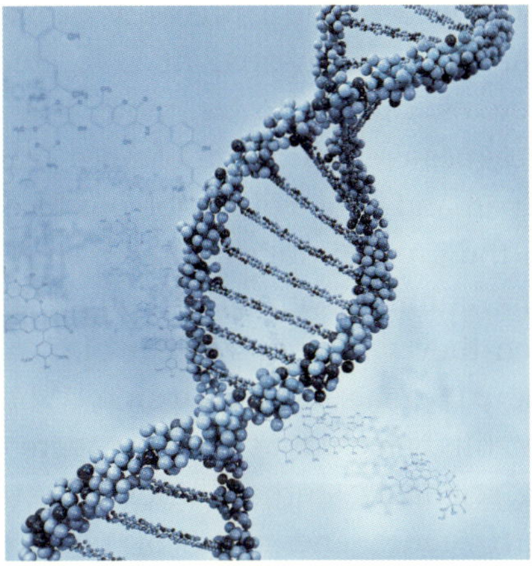

A DNA double helix

pens within one organ," explains Natalia Komarova of the University of California, Irvine.

Limits to Defenses

Although our bodies may be vulnerable to cancer, they also have many ways to halt it. These strategies probably resulted from natural selection, because mutations that made our ancestors less likely to die of cancer in their prime could have raised their reproductive success. But given the many millions of people who get cancer every year, it is obvious that these defenses have not eradicated the disease. By studying the evolution of these defenses, biologists are trying to understand why they fall short.

Tumor suppressor proteins are among the most effective defenses against cancer. Studies suggest that some of these proteins prevent cancer by monitoring how a cell reproduces. If the cell multiplies in an abnormal way, the proteins induce it to die or to slip into senescence, a kind of early retirement. The cell survives, but it can no longer divide. Tumor suppressor proteins play a vital role in our survival, but scientists have recently discovered something strange about them: in some respects, we would be better off without them.

Norman E. Sharpless of the University of North Carolina at Chapel Hill genetically engineered mice to study the effect of one of these proteins, called p16 (or, more properly, p16-Ink4a). He and his colleagues created a line of mice that lacked a functional gene for p16 and thus could not produce the protein. In September 2006 the group published three studies on the mice. As expected, the animals were more prone to cancer, which could arise when they were only a year old.

But losing the p16 gene had an upside. When the mice got old, their cells still behaved as if they were young. In one experiment, the scientists studied older mice, some of which had working p16 genes and some of which did not. They destroyed insulin-producing cells in the pancreases of the animals. The normal rodents could no longer produce insulin and

[65] **Q. prime** の意味はどれか？
1. 初期　2. 最盛期　3. 最も重要な時期

[66] **given the many millions of people who get cancer every year** = in the light of the fact that many millions of people get cancer every year. Cf. p. 40, l. 90.

[67] **Q. these defenses** とほぼ同じ意味の表現を同じ段落から探しなさい。

[70] **Q. fall short** の意味はどれか？
1. 失速する　2. 不足する　3. 目標に達しない

[71] **Q. Tumor suppressor proteins** = proteins that（　　　）a tumor

[71] **proteins** [próutiːn]**:** タンパク質

[71] **among . . .** = one（some）of . . .

[75] **senescence** [sənésns, si-]**:** 老齢、老化（期）

[79] **Q. better off without . . .** の意味はどれか？
1. 〜なしだと、より裕福な
2. 〜がないほうがいい
3. 〜なしでもより恵まれた境遇にある

[81] **Q. genetically engineered mice** はどういう意味か？

[83] **Q. a line of . . .** の意味はどれか？
1. 〜の家系　2. 一連の〜　3. 〜のラインアップ

[83] **a functional gene:** 機能遺伝子（タンパク質を作ることのできる通常の遺伝子。突然変異などでタンパク質を作れなくなったものは偽遺伝子と呼ぶ。）

[84] **Q. the protein** とは何か？

[85] **studies:** 研究論文

[86] **Q. the animals** とは具体的に何を指すか？

[86] **prone to cancer:** prone は vulnerable や susceptible の意味

[87] **Q. arise** の意味はどれか？
1. happen　2. ascend　3. wake up

[88] **an upside** =（especially American English）the positive part of a situation that is generally bad

[92] **insulin:** インシュリンは膵臓（pancreas [pǽŋkriəs]）のランゲルハンス島から分泌されるホルモン。ブドウ糖の取り込み・消費を高め、肝臓でのブドウ糖からグリコーゲンへの転換を促進することによって血糖値を低下させるはたらきがある。インシュリンの分泌異常により糖尿病（diabetes [dàɪəbíːtiːz, -tis]）が発症する。

[93] **Q. normal rodents** とはこの文脈では何を意味しているのか？

developed fatal diabetes. But the ones without the p16 protein developed only mild diabetes and survived. The progenitors of their insulin-producing cells could still multiply quickly, and they repopulated the pancreas with new cells. The scientists found similar results when they examined cells in the blood and brains of the mice: p16 protected them against cancer but also made them old.

These results support a hypothesis Campisi has developed over the past few years. Natural selection favors anticancer proteins such as p16, but only in moderation. If these proteins become too aggressive, they can create their own threats to health by making bodies age too quickly. "It's still a working hypothesis," Campisi admits, "but the data are looking stronger and stronger."

[95] **progenitors of their insulin-producing cells:**「インシュリンを生みだす細胞」の前駆細胞（幹細胞から特定の体細胞等に分化する前の細胞）

[97] **repopulated** ⇐ repopulate = re + populate

[102] Q. **anticancer** はどういう意味か？

[103] **in moderation** = moderately

[105] **working hypothesis:** 作業仮説。『広辞苑』（第 6 版）によれば、「ある一定の現象に最終的な説明を与える目的で設ける仮説ではなくて、研究や実験の過程においてそれを統整したり容易にしたりするために、有効な手段としてたてる仮説」。

14

Evolved for Cancer?

(Part 2)

Carl Zimmer

Recent research suggests that natural selection may have altered genes in ways that make cancer cells more dangerous. Evolutionary biologists discovered this disturbing possibility as they searched for the changes that have made us uniquely human. After our ancestors diverged from other apes about six million years ago, they experienced natural selection as they adapted to a new way of life as a tool-making, savanna-walking hominid. Scientists can distinguish between genes that have not changed significantly since the origin of hominids and those that have undergone major alteration as a result of selection pressures. It turns out that among the genes that have changed most dramatically are some that play important roles in cancer.

Scientists suspect that the adaptive advantages brought by these genes outweigh the harm they may cause. One of these highly evolved cancer genes makes a protein called fatty acid synthase (FAS). Normal cells use the protein encoded by this gene to make some of their fatty acids, which are used for many functions, such as building membranes and storing energy. In tumors, however, cancer cells produce FAS protein at a much higher rate. The protein is so important to them that blocking the activity of the gene can kill cancer cells. By comparing the sequence of the FAS gene in humans and other mammals, Mary J. O'Connell of Dublin City University and James McInerney of the National University of Ireland found that the gene has

[3] Q. **disturbing** はどういう意味か？ 55 ページ注 [41] を参照のこと。

[4] Q. **uniquely human** の意味はどれか？
1. 比類なくすばらしい
2. 他の動物とは異なっている
3. 人間性という独自のものをもっている

[5] Q. **diverged from other apes** はどういう意味か？

[7] Q. **a tool-making, savanna-walking hominid** [hɔ́mənid | hɑ́-] = a hominid that made (　　　) and walked in savannas (hominid: 原人)

[10] Q. **major** の意味はどれか？
1. 重要な　　2. 成人の　　3. 多数派の

[10] **selection pressures:** 淘汰（選択）圧。ある特徴をもった個体の数を増加（減少）させるよう、自然選択に一定の方向性を与える圧力。

[13] Q. **adaptive advantages** = advantages that help individuals (　　　) and leave more offspring. Cf. p. 74, l. 92.

[13] Q. **the adaptive advantages ... outweigh the harm** とは、要するにどういうことか？（105 ページ注 [57] を参照のこと。）

[14] Q. **these genes** は何を指すか？

[15] **fatty acid synthase** [sínθeis, -θeiz]**:** 脂肪酸生成酵素。生成酵素（シンターゼ）は、物質の合成反応を触媒する酵素。

[16] **encoded** ⇐ encode　文字どおりには「符号化する、暗号化する」(code = 暗号)。ここでは、遺伝子情報をもとに一定の構成・構造をもったタンパク質を作る、という意味。Cf. l. 94.

[18] **membranes** [mémbrein]**:** 膜

[22] **sequence:** (DNA の) 塩基配列

[22] Q. **the FAS gene** = the gene that (　　　) FAS

undergone strong natural selection in humans. "This gene has really changed in our lineage," McInerney says.

McInerney cannot say what FAS does differently in humans, but he is intrigued by a hypothesis put forward by the late physiologist David Horrobin in the 1990s. Horrobin argued that the dramatic increase in the size and power of the human brain was made possible by the advent of new kinds of fatty acids. Neurons need fatty acids to build membranes and make connections. "One of the things that might allow a larger brain size was our ability to synthesize fats," McInerney speculates. But with that new ability may have come a new tool that cancer cells could borrow for their own ends. Cancer cells may, for example, use FAS as an extra source of energy.

Many fast-evolving cancer genes normally produce proteins in tissues involved in reproduction—in the placenta, for example. Bernard Crespi of Simon Fraser University in British Columbia and Kyle Summers of East Carolina University argue that these genes are part of an evolutionary struggle between children and their mothers.

Natural selection favors genes that allow children to draw as much nourishment from their mothers as possible. A fetus produces the placenta, which grows aggressively into the mother's tissue and extracts nutrients. That demand puts the fetus in conflict with its mother. Natural selection also favors genes that allow mothers to give birth to healthy children. If a mother

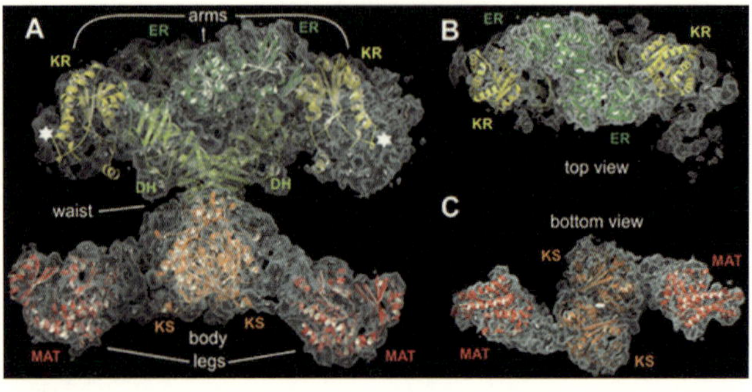

A comparison of the structure of a polyketide synthase (PKS) module with vertebrate fatty acid synthase (FAS) structure

[26] Q. **our lineage** とは、何の系譜か？
1. 人間　2. 霊長類　3. ヨーロッパ人

[28] **intrigued by** = interested in

[29] **David Horrobin:** デイヴィッド・ホロビン（1939–2003）。イギリス生まれの生理学者。アカデミックな著作のほかに多数の科学啓蒙書を残した。

[31] **advent** = arrival; appearance

[32] **Neurons:**【細胞生物】ニューロン、神経単位（神経細胞と神経突起の総称）

[34] **synthesize fats:** 脂肪を合成する

[36] Q. **ends** の意味はどれか？
1. 限界　2. 目的　3. 終着点

[38] **Many fast-evolving cancer genes normally produce proteins . . .** = Many fast-evolving cancer genes are the ones that, in normal conditions, produce proteins . . .　生物のそれぞれの個体は、どの細胞にも同じ遺伝子を持っていることを思い出そう。また、胎盤の形成に関わる遺伝子は（母親の腹から生まれてきた人なら）誰でも持っているが、胎児の時期以降は不活性な状態になるということを念頭に置いてこの一節を読もう。

[39] **reproduction:** 生殖

[39] **placenta** [pləséntə]**:** 胎盤

[45] **fetus** [fíːtəs]**:** 胎児

[47] **nutrients:** 栄養分

[Figure on p. 112]

polyketide synthase (PKS): ポリケチド合成酵素

vertebrate: 脊髄のある

fatty acid synthase (FAS) structure: 注 [15] を参照のこと。

sacrifices too much in the pregnancy of one child, she may be less likely to have healthy children afterward. So mothers produce compounds that slow down the flow of nutrients into the fetus.

Each time mothers evolve new strategies to restrain their fetuses, natural selection favors mutations that allow the fetuses to overcome those strategies. "It's a restrained conflict. There's a tug-of-war about how much the fetus is going to take from the mother," Crespi says.

Genes that allow cells to build a better placenta, Crespi and Summers argue, can get hijacked by cancer cells—turned on when they would normally be silent. The ability to stimulate new blood vessel formation and aggressive growth serves a tumor just as it does a placenta. "It's something naturally liable to be co-opted by cancer cell lineages," Summers says. "It sets up the opportunity for mutations to create tools for cancer cells to use to take over the body."

Yet even though activation of these usually quiet genes may make cancers more potent, natural selection may still have favored them because they helped fetuses grow. "You may get selection for a gene variant that helps the fetus get a little more from mom," Crespi says. "But then, when that kid is sixty, it might increase the odds of cancer by a few percent. It's still going to be selected for because of the strong positive early effects."

How vs. Why

Evolutionary biologists hope that their research can help in the fight against cancer. In addition to clarifying why evolution has not eradicated cancer, evolutionary biology may shed light on one of the most daunting challenges faced by oncologists: the emergence of drug-resistant tumors.

Chemotherapy drugs often lose their effectiveness against cancer cells. The process has many parallels to the evolution of resistance to antiviral drugs in HIV. Mutations that allow cancer cells to survive exposure to chemotherapy drugs enable the

[52] **compounds** [kɔ́mpaund | kɑ́m-]: 化合物
[56] Q. **restrained conflict** とはどのようなことか？
[57] **tug-of-war:** 綱引き、主導権争い
[60] Q. **get hijacked** は、この文脈では具体的に何を意味しているか？
[60] Q. **turned on** の意味はどれか？
1. 襲いかかる　2. ページをめくる　3. 活性化される
[61] Q. **when they would normally be silent** を和訳しなさい。
[62] Q. **serves a tumor** は何を意味しているか？
[64] **co-opted** ⇐ co-opt（他人のものを）勝手に使う。
Cf. hijacked（l. 60), take over（l. 66).
[64] Q. **cancer cell lineages** とはどのようなものか説明しなさい。
[69] Q. **You may get selection for a gene variant that . . .** はどういう意味か？
[72] **the odds** = chance, probability
[72] **It's still going to be selected for:** 自然選択の過程で選ばれるだろう。be selected for は「自然選択において（淘汰されず）選ばれる」という意味の、進化論で用いられる用語。反意語は be selected against となる。
[73] Q. **positive** の意味はどれか？
1. 積極的な　2. 絶対的な　3. プラスの
[78] Q. **shed light on** と類似する意味の表現を同じ段落から探しなさい。
[79] **oncologists:** 腫瘍学者
[80] Q. **drug-resistant** はどういう意味か？
[81] **Chemotherapy** [kìːmouθérəpi]: 化学療法
[83] **antiviral** [æ̀ntiváiərəl, æntai-]: 抗ウィルス性の
[83] **HIV** = Human Immunodeficiency Virus ヒト免疫不全ウィルス。AIDS の原因となる。
[83] Q. **Mutations that . . .** の that 節はどこまでか？
[84] **exposure to . . . :**（有害な物に）さらされること。ここでは癌細胞を抗癌剤で攻撃することを意味する。抗癌剤がきかなくなってくるのは、耐性ができる、つまり癌細胞が抗癌剤にさらされても survive するからである。
Cf. to protect people from harmful exposure to tobacco smoke.

tumor cells to outcompete more vulnerable cells. Understanding the evolution of HIV and other pathogens has helped scientists to come up with new strategies for avoiding resistance. Now scientists are investigating how understanding the evolution within tumors could lead to better ways of chemotherapy.

The concepts evolutionary biologists have been exploring are relatively new for most cancer biologists. Some are reacting with great enthusiasm. Andrew Simpson of the Ludwig Institute for Cancer Research in New York City, for instance, believes that deciphering the rapid evolution of certain genes could help in the fight against tumors that borrow them. "I think it's absolutely crucial to understand exactly why there is such strong selection on these genes," Simpson says. "Understanding that will give us a real insight into cancer."

Bert Vogelstein of the Howard Hughes Medical Institute also finds it useful to view cancer through an evolutionary lens. "Thinking about cancer in evolutionary terms jibes perfectly with the views of cancer molecular geneticists," he says. "In one sense, cancer is a side effect of evolution."

Some cancer specialists are leery of the entire approach, however. Christopher Benz of the Buck Institute for Age Research says that any insights from evolution should not be accepted until they are put to an experimental test the way any other hypothesis would be. "Call me skeptical," he says.

Crespi is familiar with this skepticism, and he thinks that it may emerge from the different kinds of questions evolutionary biologists and cancer biologists ask. "The people working on cancer are working on the how question, and the evolution people are working on why," he says.

Ultimately, the study of the evolution of cancer may reveal why eradicating the disease has proved so difficult. "There is no real solution to the problem," Jarle Breivik of the University of Oslo says. "Cancer is a fundamental consequence of the way we are made. We are temporary colonies made by our genes to propagate themselves to the next generation. The ultimate solution to cancer is that we would have to start reproducing ourselves in a different way."

[86] **pathogens:** 病原菌

[87] **come up with . . .** = produce . . . in response to a challenge

[92] **Andrew Simpson:** アンドルー・シンプソン。ニューヨーク市のルードヴィッヒ癌研究所役員。現在はゲノム科学や免疫学を結合させた研究に取り組んでいる。

[94] **deciphering:** decipher は「謎を解読する」が原意だが、ここでは「事情を明らかにする」という意味。

[95] **Q. tumors that borrow them** はどういう意味か？

[96] **there is such strong selection on . . . :** 〜に自然選択が強く作用する

[100] **through an evolutionary lens** = in evolutionary terms; from the viewpoint of evolution

[101] **jibes perfectly with . . . :** jibe with . . . は「〜と調和する」の意味。

[102] **molecular geneticists:** 分子遺伝学者

[104] **leery** [líəri] **of . . .** = skeptical about . . . 〜をうさん臭いと思う

[109] **Q. familiar with this skepticism** の意味はどれか？

1. この疑念に共感している
2. 疑いの声があるのを十分自覚している
3. 懐疑主義に詳しい

[118] **Q. colonies** はどういう意味か？ この表現にはどんなニュアンスが込められているか？

15

Easeful Death

(Part 1)

Mary Warnock and Elisabeth Macdonald

The Houses of Parliament (the Palace of Westminster)

In the British Parliament there have been three recent attempts, in 2003, 2004, and 2005, to legalize assisted death for those who requested it, and who were terminally ill. These attempts came through private members' bills, introduced into the House of Lords by Lord Joffe, an experienced and respected human rights lawyer. None of these Bills was proceeded with, the last being set aside in order that the issues might be examined by a Select Committee of the House. A fourth Bill was introduced in 2006 by Lord Joffe after the report of this Select Committee had been published and debated, but was not given a second reading and so lapsed.

All this parliamentary activity meant that the issues were kept

[About the Authors]

Mary Warnock: メアリー・ウォーノック（1924–2019）。イギリス生まれの倫理哲学者。1985年に女男爵の称号を授与される。主著に『生命操作はどこまで許されるか――人間の受精と発生学に関するワーノック・レポート』上見幸司訳（共同出版、1992）。

Elisabeth Macdonald: エリザベス・マクドナルドは、ロンドン大学キングズ・カレッジで法医学と倫理で修士号を得た癌の専門家で、ロンドン大学で教鞭をとっている。本章は、二人が2008年にロンドン大学出版局から出版した *Easeful Death: Is There a Case for Assisted Dying?* の序文の一節。

[2] **assisted death:** 医師の手を借りた死、すなわち安楽死のこと。

[3] **terminally ill:** 病気が終末期にある

[4] **private members' bills:** 通常イギリスでは、法律は政府が立案して国会に提出されるが、それ以外にも、個々の国会議員が提案することも許されている。日本の「議員立法」に相当する。

[4] **the House of Lords:** 貴族院。イギリスの上院。下院（庶民院）は House of Commons と呼ぶ。

[5] **Lord Joffe:** ジョフ卿（1932–）は、人権保護のために活躍し、ネルソン・マンデラの弁護士を務めたことで知られる。1999年にCBE（英国勲章）を受章し、2000年に男爵に叙せられた。2006年にはバース大学から名誉博士号を授与された。

[5] **human rights lawyer:** 基本的人権（fundamental human rights）に関わる法律や立法に関心の深い法律家。日本語の「人権派弁護士」という表現とは必ずしも一致しない。

[6] **Q. these Bills** とは何を指すか？

[6] **proceeded with . . . :** ～の立法に向けての手続きを続ける

[7] **Q. set aside** の意味はどれか？

1. 破棄する　　2. 棚上げにする　　3. 無視する

[7] **a Select Committee:**【英議会】特別委員会

[10] **a second reading:** 第2読会。立法化の手続きの一段階。法案の大枠が説明・議論され、投票で賛同が得られれば委員会に送られる。

[11] **lapsed:** 失効した、廃案になった

in the public eye, not only in the UK but overseas. However, the scope of Lord Joffe's Bills was extremely limited, in that the right to assisted dying was to be confined to those people who, being certified as of sound mind and unimpaired judgement, were terminally ill, that is, facing death within a matter of weeks or months, and who were suffering unbearable pain or distress. The fourth Bill sought to permit only assisted suicide, not euthanasia proper. That is, the Bill sought to legalize the action of a doctor who provided drugs that would enable the patient to kill himself, if he finally decided to do so, but the doctor would not be the killer (although provision was to be made so that where a patient was physically incapable of committing suicide, and satisfied the criteria set out in the Bill, a doctor might administer a lethal dose without fear of prosecution).

The question to be addressed is this: is it morally justifiable in some circumstances for a doctor or another person to end someone's life or help him to end it? And, if it is, is there a way of so changing the law that such an action may become not only morally but legally permitted? As the law stands, intentionally killing another person is murder, the most heinous offence of all, and the law prohibiting murder is often referred to as the cornerstone of the criminal law. Although suicide is no longer a crime in the UK (and never has been a crime in Scotland), assisting someone to commit suicide is a criminal offence, though the law is not implemented so as to visit the maximum sentence on someone found guilty of such an act.

There are various reasons why it has become a matter of urgency to try to find an answer to our question, even though it is by no means new. First, in an age when medical technology is constantly becoming more sophisticated, many people who die in hospital could be kept alive almost indefinitely on life support machines. For such people, death is not a matter of 'nature taking its course', but a matter of deliberate decision, not their own. There will come a time when someone, or some group of people, will decide not to resuscitate a patient if his heart fails, or will decide to give up all forms of treatment as

[14] **scope:** 適応範囲

[16] **certified:** certify A as B の形で「(医師が) A が B (の状態) であることを証明する」という意味。

[16] **of sound mind and unimpaired judgement:** of . . . は名詞を形容詞化する役割を果たしており、「〜 (の特徴) を持っている」という意味。
Cf. of great importance きわめて重要な。

[16] **Q. of sound mind** と **of unimpaired judgement** は各々どういう意味か？

[17] **a matter of** = approximately

[20] **Q. euthanasia** [jùːθənéiziə|-ʒ(i)ə] **proper:**「本来の安楽死」とは何を意味するか？ proper は名詞の後ろに置かれて、「本来の、厳密な意味での」という意味になる。

[23] **provision:** 但し書き、付則

[24] **where** = in the case where

[24] **Q. physically incapable** はどういう意味か？

[25] **set out:** 順序だてて説明する、述べる

[26] **Q. administer** の意味はどれか？
1. 管理する　2. 処方する　3. 投与する

[26] **a lethal dose:** 死に至る薬の投与。84 行目の lethal injection も参照。

[26] **Q. prosecution** とは、誰が何の理由で「起訴」されるのか？

[28] **Q. to be addressed** の意味はどれか？
1. 委託されるべき　2. 検討されるべき　3. 語りかけられるべき

[31] **so changing the law that . . . :** so〜that . . . の構文に注目。「…となるような形に〜する」というように、様態を表現している。

[32] **As the law stands:** 現在の法では。Cf. as it stands; as it is 現状では。

[33] **heinous** [héinəs] = very shocking and immoral

[35] **Q. cornerstone** はどういう意味か？

[35] **the criminal law:** 刑法

[37] **a criminal offence:** (刑法) 犯罪

[38] **implemented** ⇐ implement 施行する

[38] **visit A on B:** A を B に課する、与える (inflict, impose)

[39] **Q. such an act** とは具体的に何か？

[43] **Q. sophisticated** の意味はどれか？
1. 垢抜けた　2. 複雑精巧な　3. 技巧を凝らした

[44] **Q. indefinitely** の意味はどれか？
1. 曖昧に　2. 無限に　3. 不確定的に

[46] **Q. 'nature taking its course'** はどういう意味か？

[46] **Q. deliberate** の意味はどれか？
1. 慎重な　2. 意識的な　3. ゆったりした

[48] **resuscitate:** 蘇生させる

'futile' or unduly burdensome, and merely to keep him comfortable until he dies. The patient will have been allowed, if not helped, to die.

Secondly, in the old days, an individual doctor, working alone or with the help of a district nurse, might decide on treatment or the withdrawal of treatment, relying on his own judgement, and pretty secure that his judgement would not be questioned either by the patient or the patient's relatives. The doctor's power was immense, and he was virtually unaccountable to anyone. Now, both because of the prevalence of hospital deaths, with the inevitable involvement of teams of doctors and nurses, and more generally because it is no longer regarded as proper for doctors to exercise such unquestioned decision-making powers, every decision has to be both transparent and justifiable. The question, not whether a patient will die, but when he shall be allowed to die, has to be capable of being openly discussed. And this, of course, leads to the question whether, when it is possible, the patient himself should not have a part, even a major part, in the discussion. In these changed circumstances it is highly desirable that society (all of whose members are potential patients, and all mortal) should think clearly about whether a patient should be legally entitled to decide to die. It is a question that affects us all. It is not a clinical question, to be answered by the medical profession, but a social question for society at large.

Finally, we need urgently to consider practice in those few countries where some form of assisted death is already lawful. We need to see whether within these legislatures the consequences for society are turning out well or badly, whether there is reason to follow their lead or reject it.

In the Netherlands, when a patient is deemed to be mentally competent to make the request and mean it, and when his suffering is agreed to be severe, he may lawfully be helped to die by his doctor, either by being helped to commit suicide or, more usually, by a lethal injection administered at home by his doctor. The patient does not have to be terminally ill before he can be so helped. Since 1974, Dutch doctors have been openly pro-

[50] **Q. unduly burdensome** はわざと曖昧に表現されているが、具体的にどんな状況が暗示されているのか？

[54] **a district nurse:**【英】地区（巡回）看護師（保健師）。担当地区内の病人の家庭を訪問する。病院勤務の看護師は hospital nurse という。

[58] **Q. unaccountable** の意味はどれか？
1. 計算できない　2. 説明できない　3. 責任を負わない

[59] **Q. prevalence of hospital deaths** はどういう意味か？

[66] **the question whether . . . the patient himself should not have a part:** この not という否定形に注意。「加わるべきではないのか」と「加わるべきなのか」という日本語で比較してもわかるように、whether 節内が否定だと肯定的なニュアンスが加わる。Cf. I wonder if he isn't over fifty.

[69] **Q. potential patients** の意味はどちらか？
1. 病気になる可能性のある者
2. 潜在的に病気を抱えている者

[72] **Q. to be answered** = that（　　）be answered

[73] **Q. the medical profession** の意味はどれか？
1. 医師　2. 医術　3. 医療

[74] **at large** = as a whole

[75] **practice** = what is being done

[77] **Q. these legislatures** はどういう意味か？

[79] **Q. follow their lead** はどういう意味か？

[80] **is deemed to be** = is regarded as

[80] **Q. mentally competent** と同じ意味の表現を Session 15 の第 2 段落から選びなさい。

[81] **Q. the request** の内容が具体的に書かれている部分を指摘しなさい。

[81] **Q. and mean it** はどういう意味か？

[81] **Q. his suffering is agreed to be severe** =（　　）agrees that his suffering is severe

viding euthanasia on request, and if they were brought to court, they generally successfully pleaded necessity, to escape from a charge of murder.

This system understandably caused considerable uncertainty and anxiety among the medical profession, and in 2002 the law was changed by the introduction of the Termination of Life and Assisted Suicide (Review Procedures) Act, which regularized and legitimized the position of doctors. According to the terminology used in the Netherlands, 'euthanasia' means 'voluntary euthanasia' or 'voluntary assisted suicide'. So-called euthanasia, carried out supposedly in the best interests of the patient, but without his asking for it, is murder. (However there is some anecdotal evidence both that non-voluntary euthanasia is quite often carried out and that in hospital it is suggested to patients that they ask for euthanasia.) All cases where voluntary euthanasia has been carried out are supposed to be reported to the authorities; but the rate of reporting seems to be relatively low (just over 50 per cent), though this figure is naturally not easy to establish.

[87] Q. **they were brought to court** はどういう意味か？

[88] Q. **pleaded** の意味はどれか？
1. 嘆願した　2. 言い訳した　3. 抗弁として主張した

[93] **Review Procedures:** 再検討（見直し）手続き

[95] Q. **voluntary** の意味はどれか？
1. 自然発生的な　2. 自発的好意に基づく　3. 自らの意思で決める

[97] Q. **in the best interests of** はどういう意味か？

[99] Q. **anecdotal** [æ̀nikdóutl] **evidence** はどういう意味か？

[100] Q. **it is suggested to patients that they ask for euthanasia** はどういう意味か？

[104] Q. **naturally** の意味はどれか？
1. 自然の流れで　2. 自然に任せれば　3. 当然のことながら

[105] Q. **establish** の意味はどれか？
1. 確定する　2. 制定する　3. 設立する

16

Easeful Death

(Part 2)

Mary Warnock and Elisabeth Macdonald

Evelyn De Morgan, *Angel of Death*
(Public domain/Private collection)

In the American State of Oregon, only assisted suicide is lawful, and that only for the terminally ill. The Death with Dignity Act was first passed as a result of individual initiative in 1994. However, it was passed then by only a small majority of the state electorate, and its implementation was halted by an injunction until it was put to the vote again and passed into state law by an increased majority in 1997. (That there was a certain element of defiance in the face of pressure from Federal Government cannot be doubted.) The evidence suggests that far more people ask to be given drugs that they could use if they found

[1] **Oregon:** オレゴン。アメリカ合衆国北西部、太平洋岸の州。州都はセイレム。

[2] **and that:**「しかも」という意味のイディオム。

[2] **Q. Death with Dignity** はどういう意味か？

[3] **initiative:** イニシアチブ、すなわち州民の発案に基づき、選挙民の投票によって法令の制定・改廃などが行われる制度

[4] **Q. by only a small majority** はどういう意味か？

[5] **state electorate:** 州の有権者

[5] **implementation:** 実施

[5] **injunction:**【法律】インジャンクション。（通常、違法行為に対する）差し止め命令、禁止命令。

[8] **Q. defiance in the face of pressure from Federal Government** は何を意味するか？

[8] **Federal Government:**（アメリカ合衆国）連邦政府

[10] **Q. drugs that they could use . . .** とはどのような薬か？

their condition becoming intolerable than actually use the drugs to end their lives. There is comfort simply in having a viable option to fall back on. Lord Joffe's last Bill, the Assisted Dying for the Terminally Ill Bill, 2006, was closely modelled on the law in Oregon, where he was impressed by the way it was working when he visited with other members of the House of Lords Select Committee.

Finally, in Switzerland, there are two relevant articles in the Penal Code. Article 114 makes voluntary euthanasia illegal; but Article 115 makes it lawful to help someone commit suicide if, and only if, the motive is 'entirely honourable', for example, to bring suffering to an end. Acting under this exemption, there have grown up several voluntary organizations by joining which, for a fee, a patient may be helped to commit suicide at the time of his choice. The law does not actually require that the patient be assisted only if he is terminally ill; but this is laid down in a code of practice for the medical profession.

It is against this background of different legislatures that the debate takes place in the UK, the USA, Australia, and elsewhere in the world. However, we believe that it is necessary to exercise caution in using other legislatures as a guide to how we should legislate in the UK. Those countries or states that have liberalized their laws have done so for different reasons and may have argued sometimes from the standpoint of rights, sometimes from that of compassion. Moreover, cultural differences between countries make it hard to generalize about the possible consequences of liberalization. Yet because the debate is so widespread and diverse, it is a good time to review the arguments for and against euthanasia.

In what follows we do not confine ourselves to the narrow boundaries of Lord Joffe's Bills. For instance, his last Bill, following the example of the Oregon Death with Dignity Act (1994) was confined, as has been noted, to the legalization of assisted suicide. There is no doubt that the medical and nursing professions, hostile as many of them are to any form of assisted death, would nevertheless prefer the legalization of assisted suicide to that of euthanasia. We see no difference of principle

[12] Q. **viable** の意味はどれか？
1. 迫真の　2. 実行可能な　3. 生存可能な

[13] **fall back on:** （やむを得ず）頼る

[18] Q. **articles** はどういう意味か？

[18] **the Penal Code:** 刑法典

[22] Q. **this exemption** [igzémpʃən, eg-]「この免除規定」とは何か？

[23] **voluntary organizations:** 任意組織（団体）、すなわち共通の利害や関心を持った人々が任意に集まって作られた組織。

[23] Q. **which** の先行詞は何か？

[24] Q. **for a fee** はどういう意味か？

[26] **is laid down** ⇐ lay down 規定する、定める

[27] Q. **code of practice** の意味はどれか？
1. 法体系　2. 記号体系　3. 実務規定

[28] **against:** ここでは、「～に反対して」ではなく「～を背景として」という意味。Cf. The love story unfolds against a background of civil war. そのラヴストーリーは内戦を背景に展開する。

[30] Q. **exercise caution** はどういう意味か？

[32] Q. **liberalized their laws** はこの文脈では具体的にどういう意味か？

[38] Q. **arguments for and against euthanasia** = reasonings that (　　　) and (　　　) euthanasia

[40] **In what follows:**「本書では」（この文章は *Easeful Death* という本の序文から採られたものであることに注意）

[44] **the medical and nursing professions** = the medical profession and the nursing profession

[44] Q. **nursing profession** とは何か？

[45] Q. **hostile as many of them are** = (　　　) many of them are hostile

between the two. Whether a doctor actually administers the lethal dose by injection or places a lethal dose by his patient's bed, with instructions to take it orally, what is at stake is whether he should be able, within the law, deliberately to bring about the death of his patient in response to a serious request from the patient that he do so, and when the wish to die is rational, fixed, and immovable.

Again, the Joffe Bill sought to legalize assisted suicide only for the terminally ill. Many people have raised objections to the Bill based on the ambiguity of the phrase 'terminally ill'; for, they say, though most people understand more or less what is meant by 'terminal illness' it is not capable of a definition precise enough for the purposes of the law. However, if at the heart of the debate is the rightness or wrongness of helping someone to die who can see no value to himself and no pleasure in his future life, the principle involved seems to be the same whether that life is to be long or short. Indeed, when someone has a progressive illness for which there is no cure, the length of time over which he will deteriorate may be one of the features of his case that most makes him want to die. And if his illness is not progressive, but renders him entirely helpless and dependent, it may be the length and unchanging tedium of the future that makes him sure that death is to be preferred to such a life.

Lastly, Lord Joffe's Bill was to cover only those people who were mentally competent, and who have formally asked to die. Many of those who are opposed to the Bill use as their main argument that such voluntary euthanasia as was envisaged would lead 'inevitably' to a very different kind of euthanasia, the non-voluntary. Non-voluntary euthanasia is a concept at first sight so repugnant that it is difficult even to consider it rationally. Yet it occurs. Those in a permanent vegetative state may be deliberately caused to die; infants may be allowed to die if it is deemed to be in their best interests; and there is the suspicion that the mentally incompetent who are in hospital may be allowed or even helped to die. Even in the Netherlands, and certainly in other countries, including the UK, it is generally believed that in some cases doctors bring about the death of

[50] **at stake** = at issue; in question

[53] **that he do so:** requestの内容を示すthat節なので原形doが用いられている。前にshouldが省略されていると考えてもよい。he = a doctor

[53] **Q. and** は何と何をつないでいるか？

[55] **Again:**（文頭で）その上、さらに

[59] **Q. it** は何を指しているのか？

[59] **capable of . . . :** ～に耐えうる

E.g. the novel is capable of various interpretations.

[60] **at the heart of the debate is . . . :** 議論の核心には～がある

[63] **the principle involved** = the principle that we need to consider

[65] **Q. progressive illness** とは何か？

1. 進行性疾患
2. 近年発見された難病
3. 革新的治療が期待できる病気

[69] **tedium** [tíːdiəm]**:** 単調さ、退屈

[74] **Q. envisaged** [invízidʒd, en-] の意味はどれか？

1. 想定された　2. 直面された　3. 予言された

[75] **Q. 'inevitably'** はなぜ引用符に囲われているのか？

[78] **vegetative state:** 植物状態

their patients in consideration of their best interest, when they have not asked that this should happen, but when their sufferings seem unbearable and further treatment futile. Doctors have to make such decisions frequently and, understandably, it is difficult, if not impossible, to know how often. We need to face the issue of justifiable euthanasia in whatever form it presents itself.

As we have said, the problem of euthanasia is a social, not a medical problem. The issues are issues for us all. As the Select Committee Report put it: 'the acceptability of assisted suicide or voluntary euthanasia is an issue for society to decide.'

Nobody can doubt that it is a moral problem. The central difficulty is to devise a law that would permit euthanasia in such cases and rule out other cases that would be morally dubious or abhorrent. Lord Joffe struggled to define in detail the circumstances of legitimate euthanasia, and include such safeguards as would make it impregnable to abuse. It may be that there is little possibility of successfully drafting such a Bill. Difficult though it may be legislation has been successfully drafted abroad. What, in a particular case, constitutes a strong moral imperative, namely to relieve someone's suffering when it has become too great, may be extremely difficult to generalize so as to determine a public policy. The moral imperative will come from an essentially personal motive, namely compassion, aroused by sympathy, our engagement with others, and the particular circumstances of the case; but when a Bill is drafted, it is the general, not the particular, with which the legislator must be concerned. He must ask what will be the consequences, for society as a whole, if this law reaches the statute book. It is the difference between private morality and public policy that may form the stumbling-block in the path of anyone seeking to change the law on euthanasia. We hope that a solution may be found. For, after all, private morality and public policy are not unconnected. Good laws cannot exist unless their foundation is in morality.

[85] **their best interest:** 125 ページ注 [97] 参照。

[90] **Q. it presents itself** = it（　　　）

[98] **Q. such cases** とは、ここではどんな場合のことか？

[98] **dubious** [djúːbiəs | d(j)úː-] = questionable

[99] **abhorrent** [əbhɔ́ːrənt | æb-] ⇐ abhor 忌み嫌う

[101] **Q. impregnable to abuse** の意味はどれか？
1. 濫用されない　2. 酷使にたえる　3. 非難されない

[102] **Difficult though it may be:** 注 [45] 参照。

[104] **Q. in a particular case** の意味はどれか？
1. 特殊なケース　2. 独自のケース　3. 個別のケース

[104] **constitutes:**「構成する」という意味だが、be 動詞に置き換えて読むとよい。

[105] **imperative:** 要請、必要性

[105] **namely to relieve . . .** = that is, an imperative to relieve . . .

[108] **an essentially personal motive** = a motive that is personal in its essence（本来的に公共的なものではなく、個人の心に根ざしているような動機）

[109] **Q. engagement with others** はどういう意味か？

[111] **Q. general** と **particular** をそれぞれ言い換えている単語を同じ段落から抜き出しなさい。

[113] **Q. reaches the statute book** はどういう意味か？

17

Great Inventions

(Part 1)

John Brockman

What is the greatest invention of the past 2,000 years? Various answers to this question were collected by the website *Edge,* and published as a book in the year 2000. But before we start, here goes an old joke, retold by one of the contributors to the 2000 book, *The Greatest Inventions of the Past 2,000 Years*:

> A guy is taking a national poll on the most extraordinary invention of all time. During his travels, he finds himself in the Deep South and encounters a distinguished old gentleman rocking in his chair on the front porch of his house. The pollster approaches him and says, "Sir, if you don't mind, I would like to ask you a question for the poll I am conducting. I am interested in finding out what people consider to be the greatest invention of all time. Do you have an opinion on this?"
>
> The old gentleman scratches his head and replies, "Well, I would have to say the thermos."
>
> This baffles the pollster. "Sir, of the millions of responses I have collected, not one person has mentioned the thermos. Would you kindly tell me why that's your choice?"
>
> "That's easy," says the old guy. "You see, the thermos keeps cold things cold and hot things hot. But how does it know?"

[About the Author]

John Brockman: ジョン・ブロックマン（1941–）。アメリカのボストン生まれ。作家。専門分野は科学。科学や技術の広範な分野の最先端で働いている人々のコミュニケーションを目的として、Edge Foundation を設立した。本文 2 行目に出てくる *Edge* というウェブサイト（http://edge.org/）を運営している。本章は（最初の 5 行の紹介文を除いて）、*The Greatest Inventions of the Past 2,000 Years*（New York: Simon & Schuster, 2000）の一節。

[4] **contributors** [kəntríbjutəz|-tərz] ⇐ contribute

[6] **taking a national poll on . . . :** ～について全国世論調査を行っている。take a poll（世論調査を行う）は conduct a poll とも言う。

[8] **the Deep South:** 深南部（アメリカの最も南の諸州）。「田舎じみた場所」というお馴染みのイメージがあり、よくジョークのネタに使われる。

[8] **Q. distinguished** の意味はどれか？
1. 有名な　2. 威厳ある　3. 人並み外れた風采の

[10] **pollster:** 世論調査員

[15] **Q. scratches his head** はどういう気持ちを表しているか？

[16] **thermos:** 魔法瓶、保温ポット（a vacuum flask）。thermos はもともと商標（会社名）。

[21] **Q. But how does it know?** 何がおもしろいのか、説明しなさい。

Lenses (Gino Segre)

My choice for the greatest invention of the past two thousand years is the lens. First of all, without lenses you might not be able to read this—and, even worse, you might never have been able to read anything at all, if your vision had needed correcting. I remember Teddy Roosevelt's description of getting his first pair of glasses and suddenly having the world come into focus. Seeing clearly is, of course, no small matter, but it seems limited to pick eyeglasses as the greatest invention of the past two thousand years, so my vote is for lenses big and small, alone and combined: the lenses we use to read the universe and the intricacies of life are variations of those we use to read the written word.

I am going to start, however, with plain old spectacles. We don't really know when they first began to be used. They were not uncommon in fourteenth-century Italy, and by 1600 there were specialized artisans who carefully ground lenses, keeping their tricks secret. One of them, a Dutch spectacle maker named Lippershey, noticed that a combination of two lenses made distant objects bigger. He tried to use this discovery to get rich. He didn't succeed, but several of his two-lens devices were made. By 1609 one of them had reached a transplanted Florentine named Galileo Galilei, who was teaching at the University of Padua. He pointed his device—or telescope, as it was later called—at the night sky and looked out. He took his telescope apart, rebuilt it, improved it, and looked some more. What he saw changed our view of the world. The sun rotated around its

Galileo's telescope

[23] **Gino Segre:** ジノ・セグレ (1939–)。ペンシルベニア大学、物理学・天文学の教授。

[28] **Teddy Roosevelt:** シアドア (Theodore)・ローズヴェルト (1858–1919)。「セオドア・ルーズベルト」とも表記される。第26代アメリカ合衆国大統領 (1901–09)。1906年にノーベル平和賞を受賞した。Teddy は Theodore の愛称、ぬいぐるみの Teddy Bear はローズヴェルトが狩りに出たときのエピソードをもとに作られた。

[31] **Q. limited** のニュアンスに最も近いものはどれか？
1. 限界がある　2. 制限されている　3. 想像力に欠ける

[33] **Q. the lenses we use to read the universe** と **the lenses we use to read the intricacies of life** とは、具体的にそれぞれ何か？

[34] **intricacies:** 複雑なもの

[34] **Q. those we use to read the written word** とは何か？

[36] **Q. plain** の意味はどれか？
1. 素朴な　2. 色のついていない　3. はっきりと見える

[39] **artisans** [ɑ̀ːtizǽnz, ˊ ˊ | ɑ́ːrtiz(ə)nz]**:** 職人たち。Cf. artist 芸術家。

[39] **ground:** grind (磨く) の過去形

[41] **Lippershey:** ハンス・リッペルハイ (*c.* 1570–*c.* 1619)。オランダで活躍した眼鏡師で、望遠鏡を初めて製作した。本来は Lipperhey だが、1831年にミスタイプされた名前が誤って広まったとされる。

Hans Lippershey

[44] **Q. transplanted** はどういう意味か？

[44] **Florentine:** フィレンツェ (Florence) の人。ガリレオは10歳の頃フィレンツェに移住した。

[45] **Galileo Galilei:** ガリレオ・ガリレイ (1564–1642)。ピサ (「斜塔」で有名) 生まれの、イタリアの物理学者・天文学者。『天文対話』(1632) で地動説を展開した。

[46] **Padua:** パドヴァ。イタリア北東部の都市。

[47] **Q. looked out** の意味はどれか？
1. 注意した　2. じっと眺めた　3. 外の世界を見た

[47] **Q. took . . . apart** はどういう意味か？

axis, Venus revolved around the sun, the moon had mountains and valleys, Jupiter had four moons, and the Milky Way was made up of vast numbers of stars. It was crystal clear that the old Ptolemaic vision of the universe was wrong. Copernicus and Kepler were right, the earth was not the center of the universe, and there was no going back. We were launched on our exploration of outer space.

It is a short journey from the telescope to the microscope. Not surprisingly, they were discovered at around the same time. After all, they are both just the simple piecing together of the right two lenses in correct positions. Galileo used the telescope brilliantly, but he also peered through a microscope of sorts. He saw flies the size of sheep and spots of dirt that looked like rocks, but he did not know what to make of it. In 1665 Robert Hooke published a best-seller called *Micrographia*. The book had a series of beautiful plates in it, Hooke's rendering of what he had seen with his microscope. There was a fly's eye, mold on the leaf of a rose, a picture of a louse, and so on. All very pretty, but it did not lead to anything. The microscope was a tool in search of a problem. The problem eventually did develop, and it was nothing less than understanding the origins of life. This came into focus (no pun intended) when Anton van Leeuwenhoek in 1678 made a lens good enough to get a magnifying power close to 500. At that point, a whole rich substructure was revealed. A drop of pond water turned out to be filled with little "animalcules" swimming in it. Van Leeuwenhoek had discovered bacteria. It took another two hundred years to really understand what he had seen, but then it also took three hundred years to understand that the Milky Way was just one of many galaxies.

My candidate for the greatest invention of the past two thousand years is thus the lens, an excellent example of which we possess in the human eye. But the greatest invention of all time is the brain—which, incidentally, has managed to figure out how to use the lens it is already hooked up to and the lens it has learned how to build in its never-ending attempt to understand the universe.

[50] **axis:** 自転軸

[52] **crystal clear:** 非常に明晰な（clear を強調する慣用表現）

[53] **Ptolemaic** [tɔ̀ləméɪɪk｜tɑ-] ⇐ Ptolemy [tɔ́ləmi｜tɑ́l-] プトレマイオス。紀元2世紀の天文学者・地理学者・数学者。天動説を唱えた。

[53] **Q. vision** とほぼ同じ意味の語を、同じ段落から探しなさい。

[53] **Copernicus:** コペルニクス（1473–1543）。ポーランドの天文学者。1543年、地動説を述べた『天体の回転について』を刊行。コペルニクスの呈示した体系は、後のケプラー、ガリレイ、ニュートンらの科学革命の源泉となる。

[54] **Kepler:** ケプラー（1571–1630）。ドイツの天文学者。ニュートンの万有引力理論に影響を与え、地動説の確立に貢献。また、望遠鏡の研究によって近代的光学理論の基礎を築く。

[55] **Q. there was no going back** = now it was (　　　) to go back

[56] **outer space:** 大気圏外、宇宙空間

[59] **Q. piecing together** はどういう意味か？

[61] **peered** = looked closely or carefully at something, especially when you cannot see it clearly

[61] **Q. of sorts** はどういうニュアンスか？

1. 特殊な　2. お粗末な　3. さまざまな種類の

[63] **did not know what to make of it** = did not know how to interpret it

[63] **Robert Hooke:** ロバート・フック（1635–1703）。イギリスの科学者。光学・力学など幅広い分野で活躍。フックの法則の提唱者。

[64] ***Micrographia*:**『顕微鏡図譜』（右の図はこの本の挿絵の一例）

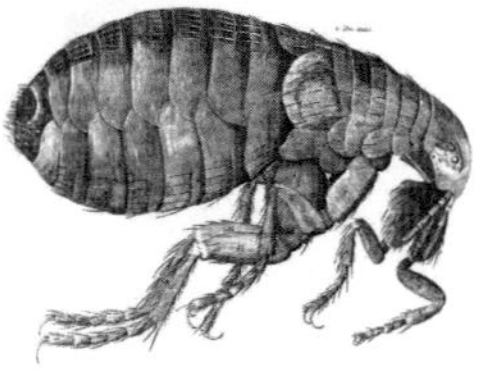

From *Micrographia*

[65] **Hooke's rendering:** フックが描いた画

[66] **mold:** 糸状菌（バラの黒星病の原因となるカビの一種）

[68] **Q. it did not lead to anything** = it got nowhere とはどういう意味か？

[70] **nothing less than . . . :** ほかならぬ〜、まさに〜

[71] **Q. no pun intended** はどういう意味か？

[71] **Anton van Leeuwenhoek** [léɪvənhùk]**:** レーウェンフック（1632–1723）。オランダの博物学者。顕微鏡を製作し、細菌や動物の精子などを発見した。

[73] **Q. 500** = five hundred (　　　)

[73] **Q. substructure** はどういう意味か？

1. 下部構造　2. 原子や分子の世界　3. 微小な生物たちの世界

[75] **animalcules** [ænəmǽlkjuːlz]**:** 肉眼ではほとんど見えない微小動物

[84] **Q. the lens it is already hooked up to** とは具体的に何のことか？

[84] **hooked up to** ⇐ hook . . . up to 〜 …を〜につなげる（取り付ける）

18

Great Inventions

(Part 2)

John Brockman

Bales of hay

Hay (Freeman Dyson)

The most important invention of the last two thousand years was hay. In the classical world of Greece and Rome, and in all earlier times, there was no hay. Civilization could exist only in warm climates, where horses could continue to graze through the winter. Without grass in winter, you could not have horses, and without horses you could not have urban civilization. Sometime during the so-called Dark Ages, some unknown genius invented hay, forests were turned into meadows, hay was reaped and stored, and civilization moved north over the

[1] **Hay:** 冬のあいだなどでも家畜に草を食べさせられるように考案された。牧草がよく育つ時期に刈り取り、天日干しをして乾燥させてから、円筒形や直方体の形に積み重ねて、納屋などで保管する。

[1] **Freeman Dyson:** フリーマン・ダイソン（1923–2020）。イギリス生まれのアメリカの理論物理学者・数学者。彗星を覆う巨大植物「ダイソン・ツリー」や宇宙植民地構想などSF的に壮大なアイデアを繰り出すアイデアマンでもある。代表的著作に『叛逆としての科学――本を語り、文化を読む22章』柴田裕之訳（みすず書房、2008）、『宇宙をかき乱すべきか――ダイソン自伝』鎮目恭夫訳（ちくま学芸文庫、2006）、『ダイソン博士の太陽・ゲノム・インターネット――未来社会と科学技術大予測』中村春木・伊藤暢聡訳（共立出版、2000）ほか。

[8] **Q. the so-called Dark Ages** にはどういうニュアンスが込められているか？

[8] **the Dark Ages:** 暗黒時代。西ローマ帝国の滅亡（476）からルネサンスに至るヨーロッパ中世のこと。

今でこそ大江健三郎と交友があり、核兵器をworst evilと認識するダイソンだが、第二次世界大戦中は'how to murder most economically another hundred thousand people'についてのエキスパートとなっていたと自ら語る（Freeman Dyson, *Weapons and Hope*, 1984）。

⇒86ページの、最も効率的にユダヤ人虐殺を行った男アイヒマンと、その世俗的批判に対するアーレントの批評を参照。

ダイソンは、広島に原爆を落としたのは、イギリスによるドイツ空爆よりも有効であり、戦争を止めてそれ以上の無駄な殺戮行為を止めるための必要悪であったという認識――多くのアメリカ人が示す認識――を示しているが、果たして我々はそのような認識を受け容れられるだろうか？

Alps. So hay gave birth to Vienna and Paris and London and Berlin, and later to Moscow and New York.

The Symphony Orchestra (Julian B. Barbour)

If it had not been invented over three thousand years ago, I should have nominated the bell, but instead I choose the symphony orchestra. This is because, like the bell, it establishes a dramatic link between two seemingly disparate worlds—the material world of science and the world of the psyche and the arts. The symphony orchestra is surely important because it made possible classical music; however, I choose it as a symbol for something that may be yet to come. Classical music is crucially dependent on physical inventions—musical instruments. I have long been fascinated by one of the great conundrums of philosophy, a conundrum that was clearly recognized by Newton's contemporaries: If there is only a material world, characterized by the so-called primary qualities, such as extension, motion, and mass, then how are we to explain our awareness of the varieties of so many secondary qualities—colors, sounds, tastes, smells? The material world has no need of them and can never explain them. Of course, we all know that science can now demonstrate that specific sensations are correlated with physical phenomena. But a correlation is not necessarily a cause—both correlates may well have a common cause—and still less is it an explanation. How can the vibrations of catgut create in me the effect I experience when listening to Beethoven's quartets?

Perhaps I am naïve. But I am also a committed scientist. I cannot be content to regard the secondary qualities as epiphenomena. I think there could be a physics, far richer than the one we know now, in which the secondary qualities are as real as, say, electric charge. The bell and the symphony orchestra call us to ponder higher things and wider possibilities, the domain where science is reconciled with the arts.

[13] **Julian B. Barbour:** ジュリアン・B・バーバー（1937–）。イギリスの理論物理学者。主著に *The End of Time: The Next Revolution in Our Understanding of the Universe*（1999）, *The Discovery of Dynamics*（2001）ほか。

[17] Q. **two seemingly disparate worlds** = two worlds that（　　　）to be separate

[20] **made possible classical music** = made classical music possible

[21] Q. **that may be yet to come** = that may come to（　　　）in future

[21] Q. **crucially dependent on . . .** はどういう意味か？

[23] **conundrums** [kənʌ́ndrəmz]**:** 難問、判じ物、なぞなぞ

[25] **contemporaries** に続くコロン（：）は that is to say（すなわち）の意味。If . . . smells? が a conundrum であることを示す。

[26] **primary qualities:** 第一性質。数量・延長・形態・固体性・運動・静止性などのように、物体自身に備わると考えられる性質。

[28] **secondary qualities:** 第二性質。色彩・温度・味など、対象そのものの性質ではなく、感覚によって知覚される性質。primary qualities とともに、イギリスの哲学者ジョン・ロック（John Locke, 1632–1704）が『人間知性論』（1689）で詳細に論じて以来、哲学上の重要な問題となった。

[31] **correlated** [kɔ́ːrəlèitid]**:** 互いに関連付けられている、相関関係にある

[32] **phenomena** ⇐ phenomenon（単数）

[33] **both correlates may well have a common cause** = it can be reasonably assumed that both correlates（相関物）have a common cause

[33] **cause:**【哲学】「原因」。運動や現象などを「引き起こすもの」という意味。

[34] Q. **still less is it an explanation** の文法構造を説明しなさい。(it = a correlation)

[34] **catgut:** ガット弦、腸弦。ただし現在の弦楽器は一般的にナイロンや金属の弦を用いているので、ここは素材と関係なく、単に弦という意味。

[37] Q. **naïve** のニュアンスはどれか？
1. 考えが単純すぎる　　2. 純真無垢の　　3. 騙されやすい

[37] Q. **committed scientist** はどういう意味か？

[38] **epiphenomena** ⇐ epiphenomenon（単数）：心理学用語で「付帯（付随、随伴）現象」などと訳される。意識は大脳活動などの物理的現象に随伴するとする考え方は epiphenomenalism（随伴現象説）と呼ばれる。脳の物理的構造や作用から人間の意識がいかに生じているかという問題（クオリアの問題）は、現在の脳科学や哲学の大きなテーマとなっている。

[39] Q. **a physics** はどういう意味か？　なぜ 'a' が付けられているのか？

[40] **real:**【哲学】実在する、現実に存在する

The Digital Bit (Terrence J. Sejnowski)

Technological advances in communication—from clay tablets to papyrus to movable type—have had a shaping influence on society, and these advances are accelerating. Almost overnight, the accumulated knowledge of the world is crystallizing into a distributed digital archive.

Images and music, as well as text, have merged into a universal currency of information, the digital bit, which is my choice for the greatest discovery of the last two millennia. Unlike other forms of archival storage, bits are forever. Clay breaks, papyrus crumbles, and paintings darken, but the information in a digital document is independent of the medium that is used to store it, and can be perfectly replicated.

In the next millennium, this digital archive will continue to expand, in ways we cannot yet imagine, greatly enhancing what a single human can accomplish in a lifetime and what our culture can collectively discover about the world and ourselves.

The Clock (W. Daniel Hillis)

I agree that science is the most important human development in the last two thousand years, but it doesn't quite qualify as an invention. I therefore propose the clock as the greatest inven-

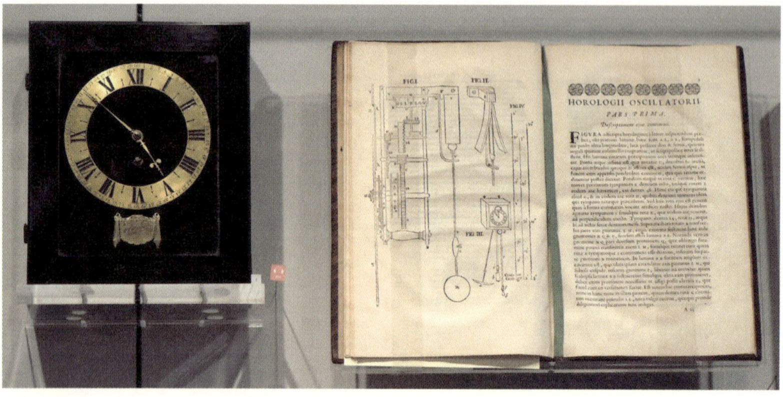

A spring-driven pendulum clock designed by Christiaan Huygens and a copy of his book *Horologium Oscillatorium* (Museum Boerhaave, Leiden)

[44] **Digital:** デジタル（型）の（⇔ analog）。すなわち、「データや物理量を離散的な数字によって表現している」という意味。

[44] **Bit:** コンピュータで用いられる情報の最小単位。2進数字の 0 か 1 を表す。

[44] **Terrence J. Sejnowski:** テレンス・J・セイノフスキー（1947–）。計算神経生物学（computational neurobiology）の先駆者。

A clay tablet with cuneiform writing

[45] **clay tablets:** 粘土板。古代メソポタミアでは、楔形文字（cuneiform [kjúːni(i)fɔ̀ːm, kjúːniː-|-fɔːrm]）を粘土板に記して乾燥させた。

[46] **papyrus** [pəpái(ə)rəs]**:** パピルス紙。古代エジプトでは、ナイル川流域の水生植物パピルスから紙を作って象形文字（hieroglyph）を書き記した。

[46] **movable type:**【印刷】組版で、それぞれが独立していて組み替えと移動のできる活字。

[46] Q. **shaping influence on society** = influence that has（　　　）society

[48] Q. **crystallizing** はどういう意味か？

[49] Q. **distributed** はどういう意味か？

[49] **digital archive:** デジタルビットによる情報の集積

[50] **have merged into . . . :** 合わさって〜になった

[51] Q. **currency** の一つの意味は「通貨」だが、ここではどういう意味か？

[53] Q. **other forms of archival storage** の具体例は何か？

[61] **W. Daniel Hillis:** W・ダニエル・ヒリス（1956–）。アメリカの発明家・文筆家・企業家。ウォルト・ディズニー・カンパニーの研究開発部門の副会長。主著に『思考する機械コンピュータ』倉骨彰訳（草思社、2000）ほか。

[63] Q. **qualify as an invention** はどういう意味か？

[Figure on p. 144]

Christiann Huygens: 53 ページ注 [Title] 参照のこと。

***Horologium Oscillatorium*:**【ラテン語】振り子時計

tion, since it is an instrument that enables science in both practice and temperament.

It was Galileo's observation of the constant period of the pendulum swing that paved the way for the invention of the pendulum clock by Christiaan Huygens in the seventeenth century. It is no coincidence that these events occurred at the beginning of the Enlightenment. Before the invention of the pendulum clock, the standard of accurate timekeeping was the sundial, which read variable hours that were long in the summer and short in the winter. Imagine trying to write Newton's laws of physics to a standard of time that varied with the season.

The clock, the embodiment of objectivity, paved the way for the rigor of objective science. It converted time from a personal experience into a reality independent of perception. It gave us a framework in which the laws of nature could be observed and quantified. The mechanism of the clock gave thinkers like Descartes and Leibniz a metaphor for the self-governed operation of natural law. The computer, with its mechanistic playing out of predetermined rules, is the direct descendant of the clock. Once we were able to imagine the solar system as a clockwork automaton, the generalization to other aspects of nature was almost inevitable, and the process of science began.

The University (Paolo Pignatelli)

My choice is the university. Knowledge increases through synergy—through the spreading activation of millions of neurons, families of neurons, and neuron families distributed among thinking individuals. Universities, in bringing individuals with a common intellectual foundation into close enough proximity to allow for rich communication, cause jumps across metaphorical collective neurons—signals that then propagate through the society of neurons and create new knowledge. Universities are about expanding our universe. Had I been asked this question two thousand years ago, my choice would have been the library.

[66] Q. **temperament** の意味はどれか？
1. 気質　2. 精神的枠組み　3. はげしい気性

[67] Q. **period** の意味はどれか？　1. 時期　2. 周期　3. 期間

[68] **paved the way for . . . :** 〜への道を開く

[70] Q. **no coincidence** とあるが、**the Enlightenment** と **the invention of the pendulum clock** にはどのような関連があるのか？

[71] **the Enlightenment:** 啓蒙運動。17–18 世紀のヨーロッパの思想運動。

[72] Q. **timekeeping** の意味はどれか？
1. 時計　2. 時間の計測　3. 時間を計る人

[73] **read:** (温度計・時計などが度・時刻などを) 示す、表示する

[74] **write . . . to 〜:** …を〜に合わせて書く

[77] Q. **rigor** の意味はどれか？　1. 過酷さ　2. 厳密さ　3. 難しさ

[80] **Descartes:** デカルト (1596–1650)。フランスの哲学者・数学者・物理学者。

[81] **Leibniz:** ライプニッツ (1646–1716)。ドイツの哲学者・数学者。

[82] **playing out:** すべて実行する

[84] **clockwork automaton [ɔːtɔ́mətn | -tɑ́m-]:** 時計じかけの自動装置

[85] Q. **generalization** の意味はどちらか？　1. 一般化　2. 一般論

[87] **Paolo Pignatelli:** 企業家。コンピュータソフトの販売などの会社を経営。

[88] **synergy:** 共同作用。例えば 2 つ以上の筋肉や神経などが一緒に作用することで相乗効果を生むこと。

[89] **millions of neurons, . . . and neuron families:** neurons は脳を構成する微細な神経の最小単位、families of neurons は個人の脳の中に存在する、運動、感覚、記憶等々のさまざまな機能を果たす単位としてのニューロンの集合体、neuron families は (なんらかの意味で共通性をもった) 複数の人間のニューロンを集合的にイメージしている。人間や社会をニューロンの集まりという観点から眺めているのである。進化生物学者のリチャード・ドーキンズが 1976 年に *The Selfish Gene* (邦題『利己的な遺伝子』) で、人間の社会を遺伝子のプールとして眺めているのと似たような発想。

[93] Q. **jumps** の意味はどれか？
1. 急上昇　2. 発想の飛躍　3. 跳ねること

[93] Q. **across** の意味はどれか？
1. 〜の全体に　2. 〜を横切って　3. 〜の向こう側に

[93] Q. **cause jumps across metaphorical collective neurons** の意味は何か？

[93] Q. **metaphorical collective neurons** の指示する内容はどれか？
1. 人類全体　2. 社会の人々　3. 大学に集まった人々

[94] **propagate:** 普及する

[96] **about . . . :** 〜に関わるもの、〜するもの。all about . . . で「〜の本質」という意味になる。E.g., Pain and tears . . . That's what love is all about.

[96] **Had I been asked . . .** = If I had been asked . . .

19

Politics, Scandal and Propaganda of Ancient Olympic Games
(Part 1)

Judith Swaddling

The approach of each modern Olympics inevitably provokes a comparison between the perceived simplicity and idealism of the original Olympics and the lavish, high-security spectacle of the modern Games. Place the ancient Games under close scrutiny, however, and we can discern elements of bribery, corruption, scandal, political intrusion, propaganda and profiteering—precisely the problems that beleaguer the modern Games.

Even before the influence of the Romans, with their love of grandiose public entertainment, the ancient Greek contests were a big news event, drawing tens of thousands of spectators and turning top athletes into living legends. The enthusiasm of the classical world for sport was such that not only was there one major Greek national Games event every year but other Greek localities sponsored smaller meets, and by Roman times hundreds of sports festivals around the Mediterranean had been granted 'Olympic' status, their events and programmes modelled closely on the original.

Fame and Wealth for the Winners

The Greeks traditionally believed that athletes received their prowess in part from the gods and therefore it was to the gods that athletes prayed for victory and offered gifts, both to curry favour and in gratitude. From as early as the fourth century BC,

[About the Author]

Judith Swaddling: ジュディス・スワドリング。British Museum に勤務する研究員。古代ギリシャ・ローマが専門。本章は、*The Ancient Olympic Games*, 2nd ed. (Austin: University of Texas Press, 2000) からの一節。

[1] Q. **The approach of . . .** の意味はどれか？
1. ～の研究方法　2. ～がやってくること　3. ～への近づき方

[1] Q. **provokes** の意味はどれか？
1. 怒らせる　2. 挑発する　3. 呼び起こす

[2] **the perceived simplicity and idealism** = what is generally believed to be the simplicity and idealism

[3] Q. **the original Olympics** とは何か？
1. 元々のオリンピック　2. 風変わりなオリンピック

[3] Q. **lavish, high-security spectacle** はどういう意味か？

[4] Q. **Place . . . under close scrutiny** はどういう意味か？

[6] Q. **political intrusion** は何を意味するか？ 近代オリンピックでの具体的な例を想起して挙げなさい。

[6] **profiteering:** 不当な暴利をむさぼること

[7] **beleaguer** [bilíːgə|-gər]**:** つきまとう。
Cf. beleaguer a town 町を包囲する。

[9] **grandiose** [grǽndìous] **public entertainment:** 壮大な大衆向けのショー（催し）。コロセウム（円形闘技場）で行われた猛獣と人間の死を賭した決闘などが有名。

[10] Q. **a big news event** とは何か？

[13] **national:** ギリシャ民族の。ここでは地中海および沿岸各地に住んでいたギリシャ人の世界全体を示している。

[13] Q. **other** が修飾する名詞は？

[14] **localities:** 都市国家や都市国家内の区（デーモス）など、ギリシャ人の世界全体より限定された地域を指す。

[14] **meets:** スポーツの競技会、大会

[14] **Roman times:** 紀元前 146 年のコリントスの戦い以降、ギリシャの都市国家はローマの支配下に入った。

[15] **the Mediterranean:** 地中海

[15] Q. **had been granted 'Olympic' status** とはどういうことか？

[17] Q. **the original** とは何か？

[20] **prowess** [práuis]**:** 並はずれた才能

[21] **curry favour:**「加護を求める」という意味の熟語。しばしば「機嫌をとる」、「お世辞を言う」といった否定的な文脈で用いる。

[21] Q. **to curry favour** と **in gratitude** は、この文脈で具体的にどのようなことを意味しているか？

however, the inscriptions on the stone bases of the victors' statues begin to tell us a different story: it was already the athletes themselves and their city-states who were receiving primary recognition.

At the major games the only prizes were symbolic honours: crowns of olive at Olympia, laurel at Delphi, fresh celery and later pine at Corinth, and dried celery at Nemea. The victors' home states, however, provided ample cash rewards, along with such civic honours as free board and lodging and theatre seats, not to mention, by the third and second centuries BC, extravagant receptions and parades. The Athenian legislator Solon had decreed that Athenian winners at the Isthmian and Olympic Games should receive cash rewards—100 drachmai for Isthmian and 500 drachmai for Olympic victories (an income of 500 drachmai per annum would have placed an Athenian in the top earning bracket). Sometimes states would erect statues of their victors at the location where they won their victories or in their hometown. This was no mean reward, for a life-size statue in bronze or marble could cost the equivalent of ten years' wages for the average worker. Doubtless some of the wealthier victors financed their own monuments: one man, Dikon, had fifteen

Lancelotti Discobolus

[25] **city-states:** 都市国家

[25] **Q. receiving primary recognition** はどういう意味か？

[27] **Q. symbolic honours** と対立する表現を、同じ段落から選びなさい。

[28] **crowns of . . . :** olive, laurel, fresh celery など、後に続く一連の植物を修飾する。

[28] **Olympia:** オリンピア。古代ギリシャ、ペロポネソス半島西部の平原に位置した。古代オリンピック発祥の地。

[28] **Delphi:** デルフォイ、デルポイ。古代ギリシャの時代にはアポロの神託地として栄えた。

[29] **Corinth:** コリント、コリントス。ギリシャ南部、ペロポネソス半島北東部の港町。

[29] **Nemea:** ネメア。古代ギリシャの南東部の谷の町で、ネメア祭が行われた。

[30] **Q. states** = (　　　)-states

[31] **Q. free board and lodging** はどういう意味か？

[33] **Solon:** ソロン (*c.* 638–*c.* 558 bc)。古代アテネの政治家。

[34] **Isthmian** (⇐ isthmus 地峡): コリント地峡の、イストミア祭の

[35] **drachmai** ⇐ drachma (単数): ドラクマ (古代ギリシャの銀貨)

[37] **per annum** [pər ǽnəm | pə(ː)ǽnəm]: 【ラテン語】1 年につき (per year)

[38] **bracket:** (所得の) 範囲、階層

[40] **Q. mean** の意味はどれか？

1. 下品な　　2. ささやかな　　3. 身分の低い

Tetradrachm of Syracuse, around 450–405 bc

statues, equal to his number of Olympic wins.

States would sometimes pay for an athlete's training, and there are even instances of top athletes being 'bought' by city-states that hoped to benefit from athletic or equestrian triumphs. The wealthy Greek colonies of southern Italy and Sicily had a very strong penchant for sports, in which they invested heavily, particularly in the equestrian events and by recruiting athletes from other cities. In the early fifth century BC, Astylos of Croton (in southern Italy), victor in the long-distance race and in the race-in-armour, mysteriously changed his national allegiance to Syracuse (in Sicily) between one Olympics and the next, while in the fourth century BC, a Syracusan tyrant tried to bribe the father of a winner in the boys' boxing contest to have the boy proclaimed a Syracusan. Similarly, the city of Ephesus in Asia Minor succeeded in acquiring a Cretan long-distance runner after his second Olympic victory.

While the expense of maintaining horses and equipping a team meant that only the wealthy could compete in chariot races, a young athlete from the lower classes could probably work his way up to the top in other athletics events. The first known Olympic victor, Koroibos, is recorded as a cook, while other early victors included a cowherd and a goatherd. There were no regulations prohibiting professional athletes from competing at the ancient games, and a successful athlete probably could have earned his living simply by travelling around from one athletics event to another. While cash prizes were not given at the Olympics themselves, elsewhere a single sprint race could earn the winner a prize large enough to buy a luxury house.

A chariot

[47] **equestrian** [ikwéstriən]: 馬術の。Cf. equine [íːkwaɪn, ék-] 馬の。

[48] **Sicily:** シチリア島。イタリア半島南西端西方にメッシナ海峡を隔てて位置する地中海最大の島。

[49] **penchant** [péntʃənt] = a strong and continued inclination; liking

[51] **Croton:** クロトン。イタリア本土の南端にあったギリシャの植民都市。オリンピックの勝者を輩出したことで有名。

[53] **race-in-armour:** 甲冑を着て行う競走。それ以外の競走は素はだかで行われた。

[53] **Q. mysteriously**（「不思議なことに」）は何を暗示しているのか？

[53] **changed national allegiance:**「国家への忠誠を変えた」とは、「国籍を変えた」ということ。

[54] **Syracuse:** シュラクサイ。シチリア島東部にあったギリシャの植民都市。現在のシラクサ。

[57] **Ephesus:** エフェソス、エペソ。小アジア西部のイオニアの古都。

[57] **Asia Minor:** 小アジア（黒海と地中海に挟まれたアジア西部の半島）

[58] **Cretan:** クレタ人の

[61] **chariot:**（古代エジプト・ギリシャ・ローマなどの）一人乗り軽二輪戦車

[63] **Q. work his way up** の意味はどれか？

1. 坂道を上がっていく
2. アスリートとして伸びる
3. 上の身分へと上がっていく

[63] **Q. other athletics events** とは何か？ 何に対して 'other' なのか？

[71] **luxury:**（形容詞として）ぜいたくな、豪華な、高級な

Celebrity sportsmen were occasionally paid huge fees by entrepreneurs to appear at local festivals, in one case as much as five talents, the equivalent of about 27 kg of silver. At the Great Panathenaic festival in Athens, held every four years in honour of Athena, patron goddess of the city, vast quantities of olive oil were presented as prizes. The olive oil was contained in amphorae decorated with illustrations of the goddess Athena on one side and the contest at which the prize was won on the other. The oil was used for lighting, heating and cooking, and for cleansing and lubricating the body. The vessels, with or without oil, were occasionally sold, often to buyers in Italy. Athletes were apparently allowed to export vessels without paying the usual duty. Each vessel was worth a minimum of twelve days' wages, and the biggest prize, for the sprint, was one hundred amphorae with an estimated value of many thousands of pounds.

Famous poets, notably Pindar the great Greek lyricist, were paid large sums to write songs in the victors' honour. Wins were recorded with pride—on athletes' epitaphs and in stone inscriptions that hailed them as benefactors of the state. The names of the winners in the Olympic foot-race were even used as a dating system for the four-year periods, or Olympiads, by tradition going back to 776 BC. In this respect it is essential to remember that the prime objective at the ancient Olympics was to come first: second or third places counted for nothing and were not even recorded.

[72] **Celebrity sportsmen:** 高名なスポーツ選手たち

[72] **entrepreneurs** [ɔ̀ntrəprənə́ːz | ɑ̀ːntrəprə́nərːz]**:** persons who organize, manage, and assume the risks of a business or enterprise

[74] **talents** ⇐ talent（単数）**:** タラント。古代ギリシャ・ローマの貨幣・重量単位。

[75] **Panathenaic** ⇐ Panathenaea**:** 全アテネ祭。女神アテナに捧げられた祭典。古代アテネで 4 年毎に行われた（例祭は毎年）。

[76] **Athena:**【ギリシャ神話】アテナ。知恵、豊穣、工芸、戦術の神として崇拝された女神。

[76] Q. **patron goddess** とは何か？

[78] **amphorae** ⇐ amphora（単数）**:**【古代ギリシャ・ローマ】アンフォラ。大型の両取っ手付き卵形の壺。主として油やぶどう酒を入れるのに用いられた。

An amphora

[81] **lubricating** ⇐ lubricate 油を塗る

[81] Q. **vessels** とは何か？ 同じ段落の語で言い換えなさい。

[84] Q. **duty** の意味はどれか？
1. 関税　2. 義務　3. 職務

[88] **Pindar:** ピンダロス（*c*. 522–*c*. 443 BC）。ギリシャの抒情詩人。代表作に『競技祝勝歌』がある。

[90] **epitaphs:** 墓碑銘

[91] Q. **benefactors** の意味はどれか？
1. 恩人　2. 後見人　3. 寄付者

[92] **used as a dating system:** 勝者の名がちょうど年号のように用いられ、「～が勝者となってから X 年めのこと」などというように暦が表現されたということ。

[93] **Olympiads:** オリンピアード、オリンピア紀。あるオリンピア競技会が開催されてから次の競技会が開催されるまでの 4 年間のこと。年を特定するため「第～オリンピアードの第 X 年」と数えた。

[95] Q. **come first** の意味はどれか？
1. 早い者勝ち　2. いち早く帰る　3. 1 等になる

[96] Q. **counted for nothing** の意味はどれか？
1. 意味がないとみなされた　2. ゼロとして計算された

20

Politics, Scandal and Propaganda of Ancient Olympic Games

(Part 2)

Judith Swaddling

Politics and Sport

The national sanctuaries were cultural and religious centres that provided arenas not only for sporting events but also for music, dance, drama and public debate. Olympia was crammed with temples and altars to the gods, as well as treasury buildings where city-states and colonies could display their wealth; and to impress visitors, states erected monuments to their deities, athletes, statesmen, heroes and military triumphs. Although the Eleans, in whose territory the sanctuary of Olympia was situated, were of minor political significance, they inevitably became embroiled in hostilities as a result of their role in the festival, and the problems of this are documented from at least as early as the fifth century BC.

The ancient gymnasia and sports festivals were ideal as political forums, and often statesmen used the occasion of the Olympic festival to deliver an oration to the assembled masses. The admiral Themistokles enjoyed a spectacular welcome at the first Olympic festival after the Persian Wars, which had culminated in his victory at the Battle of Salamis in 480 BC. He so captured the admiration of the assembled crowds that for the rest of that day it was he who had their attention rather than the Games. The historian Herodotos also read his account of the Persian Wars here. Here, too, in 388 BC Lysias delivered his

[2] **sanctuaries:** 神聖な場所、聖地

[8] **the Eleans:** エリア人。本文では、古代ギリシャ、ペロポネソス半島北西部の地方で、古代オリンピックの開催地 Elis（Eleia）の形容詞形として Elean が用いられている。

[10] Q. **minor** の意味はどれか？
1. 小さな　2. 未熟な　3. 少数派の

[11] Q.（be）**embroiled in hostilities** はどういう意味か？

[14] **gymnasia** [dʒimnéɪziə] ⇐ gymnasium: 練成所、体育場、ギュムナシオン（古代ギリシャの青年が集まって運動や討論をした場所）

[15] **forums:** 公開討論の場、討論会場

[16] **deliver an oration:** 演説を行う

[16] Q. **the assembled masses** はこの場合はどちらを意味するか？
1. 集められた選手たち　2. 集まった大勢の人々

[17] **admiral** [ǽdm(ə)rəl]: 提督。近代的に表記するなら、役割的名称としては「艦隊司令長官」、階位としては「大将」を意味するが、一般に海軍のトップクラスの軍人の尊称として用いられる。Cf. general.

[17] **Themistokles:** テミストクレス（*c.* 528–*c.* 462 bc）。アテネの将軍・政治家。前 480 年にサラミスの海戦（Battle of Salamis）でペルシャ軍を破った。右写真。

Themistokles

[18] **the Persian Wars:** ペルシャ戦争。ギリシャとペルシャ帝国とのあいだの戦争（499–449 bc）。マラトン（Marathon）の会戦（490 bc）、サラミス（Salamis）の海戦（480 bc）などが有名。

[22] **Herodotos**（= Herodotus）**:** ヘロドトス（*c.* 484–*c.* 425 bc）。ギリシャの歴史家。代表作は『歴史』。

[22] **read his account:** 記述を朗読した（read = read aloud）

[23] **Lysias:** リシアス（*c.* 450–*c.* 380 bc）。古代ギリシャの法廷弁論代作者。

'Olympic Oration', through which he succeeded in persuading the Greeks to rout his fellow-countryman, the tyrant Dionysios of Syracuse, who had wreaked havoc and destruction after seizing control of the whole of south-western Italy. Dionysios had sent several teams of horses to be entered at the Games, professional speakers to recite his poems, and a tent decorated with golden thread and furnished with vivid carpets to house his delegates. As an immediate response to Lysias' incitement, the crowd opened hostilities by creating uproar during the recitals and by looting the magnificent tent.

Athletes themselves occasionally served as political envoys or, like the modern British runner Sebastian Coe, took up politics after their retirement. Such was the case of Theagenes of Thasos, a boxer and wrestler who ventured into public affairs after a stunning sports career spanning more than twenty years, with twenty-three victories in the circuit games and more than a thousand at lesser festivals. Unfortunately, his successes, if not the rigours of his sport, seem to have gone to his head, for he also began to proclaim himself the son of the demi-god Herakles.

Opportunities for Sponsorship and Self-Advertisement

Equestrian events were the showiest and most magnificent and provided ample opportunities for propaganda. Sometimes chariot entries were financed not by individuals but by states: in 472 BC, for example, the 'public chariot' of the Argives won an Olympic victory. The investment was good publicity for a state that specialized in horse-breeding. The extensive plains of Argos, Euboea and Thessaly and the area around Athens were renowned for their breeds of horses, but most famous of all were those of Sicily and southern Italy. In those parts horse sports were the passionate love of the local princes. They tried to gain popularity and influence with the crowds at major festivals by entering teams of horses in the Games and making numerous dedications, and to ensure victory it was not unusual for an individual to enter a number of chariots in one race. In

[25] **rout** [ráut]**:** 打ち破る、敗走させる

[25] **fellow-countryman:** 同国人、同胞

[25] **Dionysios:** ディオニシオス（1 世）（*c.* 430–367 bc）。シチリア島シュラクサイの僭主。カルタゴ勢力と戦ってシチリア島の大半を支配下におさめ、イタリア方面にも進出した。自ら悲劇を書くなど学芸も好み、哲学者プラトンをその宮廷に招いた。

[26] Q. **wreaked havoc** はどういう意味か？

[30] Q. **house** の意味はどれか？
1. 貯蔵する　2. 収容する　3. 避難所を与える

[31] **delegates:** 使節、代表団。34 行目の envoys も同じ意味。

[31] Q. **incitement** の意味はどれか？
1. 激励　2. 煽動　3. 動機

[32] Q. **recitals** の具体的な内容を説明している箇所を指摘しなさい。

[33] **looting** ⇐ loot 略奪する

[35] **Sebastian Coe:** セバスティアン・コー（1956–）。イギリスの陸上選手。1980 年、84 年のオリンピックの 1500 m 走で金メダルを獲得し、1990 年に引退、1992 年に保守党の国会議員になった。

[36] **Theagenes of Thasos:** タソス島のテアゲネス。紀元前 5 世紀の人。

[37] Q. **ventured into public affairs** と実質的に同じ意味の表現を同じ段落から選びなさい。

[39] **the circuit games:** 回り持ちでさまざまな場所で開催された競技会

[41] Q. **rigours** [rígəz | rígərz] の意味はどれか？
1. 厳しさ、苦しさ　2. 厳密さ　3. 筋肉の硬直

[41] Q. **gone to his head** の意味はどれか？
1. 頭にきた　2. 我を忘れさせた　3. のぼせ上がらせた

[43] **Herakles** (= Hercules)**:**【ギリシャ神話】ヘラクレス。ゼウスが人間とのあいだに儲けた半神で、怪力無双の英雄。

[48] **Argives:**（古代ギリシャの）アルゴス（Argos）人たち

[49] Q. **good publicity** はどういう意味か？

[51] **Argos:** アルゴス。ギリシャ南東部、アルゴリス湾に臨む古代都市。

[51] **Euboea:** エウボイア島。エーゲ海西部に浮かぶ島。

[51] **Thessaly:** テッサリア。古代ギリシャ北東部の地方。

[54] **local princes:** 地方の領主。prince は小国の統治者。

[57] **dedications:** 奉納、寄付

[58] Q. **for an individual to enter a number of chariots in one race** はどういう意味か？

416 BC the Athenian politician Alkibiades entered seven chariots at the Olympic Games, taking first, second and either third or fourth place. Alkibiades' enemies—and he had many—levelled all kinds of charges against him, including one of taking a fellow-competitor's horses. At the time Alkibiades was seeking generalship in a proposed invasion of Sicily, and retaliated strongly, claiming that, whereas non-Athenian Greeks had thought Athens to be weakened by the Peloponnesian War, they now believed Athenian power was greater than it actually was because of his exceptional performance at the Olympic Games, and that this was of great political benefit to the state. Political propaganda is by no means peculiar to the modern Olympics.

Alkibiades was not the only Athenian general addicted to chariot-racing. Cimon, the father of the great Miltiades, won the four-horse chariot-race at three successive Olympic Games, in 532, 528 and 524 BC. His horses were honoured not only with bronze statues but with burial in the family tomb.

Were the Judges beyond Suspicion?

As for bribery, there is indisputable evidence from antiquity of corruption among a minority of competitors and of the severe punishment with which such instances were met, but there is only one known occasion where the judges themselves were compromised. Contrary to the present situation, the Olympics had a permanent home, and so there were no inducements offered to the judges and officials by would-be hosts. Such was the concern for impartiality in the Olympic administration that, as Herodotos relates, in the early sixth century BC a delegation from Elis visited the Pharaoh Psammis in Egypt seeking advice on how to improve the organization of the Games. After consultation with his advisers Psammis proffered that true impartiality could only be achieved if the Eleans themselves were excluded from the Games. It is uncertain whether this proposal was ever adopted, and it is a little surprising that until the fourth century BC the judges were allowed to enter horses in the equestrian events. In 372 BC, however, when the Elean Troi-

Alkibiades

[59] **Alkibiades** (= Alcibiades [ælsəbáiədiːz]): アルキビアデス (*c.* 450–404 bc)。アテネの政治家・将軍。ペロポネソス戦争でスパルタの艦隊を撃破した。右写真。

[61] **Q. he had many** = he had many (　　　)

[61] **Q. levelled** の意味はどれか？
1. 平らにする
2. 浴びせる
3. 根こそぎ破壊する

[62] **Q. charges** はどういう意味か？

[62] **one** = a charge

[63] **Q. seeking generalship** の意味はどれか？
1. 将軍の名前に憧れていた
2. 司令官から優遇されていた
3. 司令官になりたがっていた

[64] **Q. retaliated** は何に対して「応酬した」のか？ 同じ段落から抜き出しなさい。

[66] **the Peloponnesian War:** ペロポネソス戦争 (431–404 bc) は、アテネとスパルタ間で繰り広げられた。

[68] **Q. exceptional** の意味はどれか？
1. 番外の　　2. まれに見る　　3. 非難に値する

[72] **Cimon** [kímən | sáimən]: キモン (*c.* 585 bc–after 528 bc)。アテネの政治家。三度オリンピックの chariot race で優勝したが、暗殺された。

[72] **Miltiades:** ミルティアデス (*c.* 540–489 bc)。アテネの将軍。マラトンの戦いでペルシャ軍を撃破 (490 bc)。

[77] **Q. from antiquity** とは何を意味するか？

[78] **Q. minority** の意味はどれか？
1. 少数　　2. 未成年　　3. 少数集団

[80] **Q. judges** の意味はどれか？
1. 審判　　2. 鑑定家　　3. 裁判官

[81] **Q. compromised** (⇐ compromise) のこの文脈での意味はどれか？
1. 譲歩した　　2. 妥協した　　3. 不正をはたらいた

[82] **Q. a permanent home** とはどこか？

[83] **Q. would-be hosts** の意味はどちらか？
1. 開催希望地 (希望者)　　2. 将来の開催地 (開催者)

[86] **the Pharaoh** [féərou, fǽ-, féi-] **Psammis** [sáməs] (Psammeticus, Psammetichus): エジプト王プサメティクス 2 世 (595–589 bc)

[88] **proffered** = proposed

los won victories in both the two-horse chariot race and the four-horse colts' race, the Eleans finally decided to ban judges' horses from the competitions.

The awe and respect in which the Elean authorities were generally held seems to have precluded any unwarranted interference, with onc notorious exception. The Emperor Nero had the Games postponed from AD 65 to AD 67, and appeared with a ten-horse team, only to be thrown from his chariot. He was helped to remount but still failed to finish, yet even so he was proclaimed victor, on the grounds that he would have won had he been able to complete the course. Matters were, however, rectified: after his death in AD 68 the Games were declared invalid and Nero's name was expunged from the victor-lists. His successor Galba also insisted that a 250,000-drachma bribe to the judges, to whom Nero had also awarded Roman citizenship, should be paid back.

[95] **colts:** 子馬（複数）

[98] **Q. unwarranted interference** の意味はどちらか？
1. 不当な介入　　2. ルールにはない裁定

[99] **Nero:** ネロ（37–68）。ローマ皇帝（在位 54–68）。

[105] **rectified** ⇐ rectify = to correct something that is wrong

[106] **Q. invalid** [invǽlid] はどういう意味か？

[106] **expunged** ⇐ expunge 抹消する

[107] **Galba:** ガルバ（*c.* 5 bc–ad 69）。Nero 暗殺のあとを継いだローマ皇帝（在位 68–69）。即位後まもなく暗殺された。

A relief featuring a chariot race

21

Miss Pinkerton's Apocalypse

(Part 1)

Muriel Spark

One evening, a damp one in February, something flew in at the window. Miss Laura Pinkerton, who was doing something innocent to the fire, heard a faint throbbing noise overhead. On looking up, 'George! come here! come quickly!'

George Lake came in at once, though sullenly because of their quarrel, eating a sandwich from the kitchen. He looked up at the noise then sat down immediately.

From this point onward their story comes in two versions, his and hers. But they agree as to the main facts; they agree that it was a small round flattish object, and that it flew.

'It's a flying object of some sort,' whispered George eventually.

'It's a saucer,' said Miss Pinkerton, keen and loud, 'an antique piece. You can tell by the shape.'

'It can't be an antique, that's absolutely certain,' George said.

He ought to have been more tactful, and would have been, but for the stress of the moment. Of course it set Miss Pinkerton off, she being in the right.

'I know my facts,' she stated as usual, 'I should hope I know my facts. I've been in antique china for twenty-three years in the autumn,' which was true, and George knew it.

The little saucer was cavorting round the lamp.

'It seems to be attracted by the light,' George remarked, as one might distinguish a moth.

Promptly, it made as if to dive dangerously at George's head.

[About the Author]

Muriel Spark: ミュリエル・スパーク（1918–2006）。スコットランド生まれのイギリスの小説家。前衛的、実験的な作風によって名声を得た。代表作に *Memento Mori*（1959）、*The Prime of Miss Jean Brodie*（1961）、*The Driver's Seat*（1970）などがある。ここに収録した短編小説は1958年の作品。

[Title] **Apocalypse:** 'the Apocalypse' といえば聖書の「黙示録」のことだが、この書物が最終的な神の目的を明らかにし、終末を描いているところから、派生的に「（全面的、壊滅的な破壊による）世界の終わり」という意味で用いられる。

[2] Q. **doing something innocent to the fire** とはどういうことか？

[3] Q. **On looking up** = The instant (　　　) looked up, (　　　) said,

[10] **flattish** (= flat + ish): 形容詞に -ish をつけることによって「〜っぽい」といった、ぼやかすようなニュアンスが出る。
Cf. fourish 4時頃、greyish 灰色がかった。

[11] Q. **eventually** は「ようやく、やっとのことで」という意味だが、この表現から George のどういう心理が読み取れるだろうか？

[12] **an antique piece:** 骨董品

[15] Q. **He ought to have been more tactful . . . :** すなわち、George was not tactful ということが含意されているが、George の直前のセリフのどこが tactful でないのだろうか？

[15] Q. **would have been** = would have been (　　　)

[16] Q. **but for the stress of the moment** = (　　　) it had not been (　　　) the stress of the moment

[16] **set Miss Pinkerton off** = made Miss Pinkerton angry or excited

[17] Q. **she being in the right** = (　　　) she was right

[18] Q. **I should hope** は I hope とどう違うのか？

[19] Q. **I've been in antique china** の意味はどちらか？
1. 古代中国に興味がある　　2. 骨董の陶器を商ってきた

[21] **cavorting** ⇐ cavort [kəvɔ́ːrt]【口語】はねまわる、はしゃぎまわる

[22] **as one might distinguish a moth** = as one might distinguish a moth from other flying things

[24] **make as if to . . . :** （〜しそうな）そぶりを見せる

He ducked, and Miss Pinkerton backed against the wall. As the dish tilted on its side, skimming George's shoulder, Miss Pinkerton could see inside it.

'The thing might be radioactive. It might be dangerous.' George was breathless. The saucer had climbed, was circling high above his head, and now made for him again, but missed.

'It is not radioactive,' said Miss Pinkerton, 'it is Spode.'

'Don't be so damn silly,' George replied, under the stress of the occasion.

'All right, very well,' said Miss Pinkerton, 'it is not Spode. I suppose you are the expert, George, I suppose you know best. I was only judging by the pattern. After the best part of a lifetime in china—'

'It must be a forgery,' George said unfortunately. For, unfortunately, something familiar and abrasive in Miss Pinkerton's speech began to grind within him. Also, he was afraid of the saucer.

It had taken a stately turn, following the picture rail in a steady career round the room.

'Forgery, ha!' said Miss Pinkerton. She was out of the room like a shot, and in again carrying a pair of steps.

'I will examine the mark,' said she, pointing intensely at the saucer. 'Where are my glasses?'

Obligingly, the saucer settled in a corner; it hung like a spider a few inches from the ceiling. Miss Pinkerton adjusted the steps. With her glasses on she was almost her sunny self again, she was ceremonious and expert.

A Spode cup-and-saucer set

[25] Q. **ducked** の意味はどれか？
1. クワッと叫んだ　2. よたよたした　3. ひょいと頭を下げた

[26] **tilted on its side:** 横に傾いた

[26] Q. **skim** は「スキム・ミルク」の skim だが、ここではどういう意味か？

[29] Q. **breathless** のニュアンスはどれか？
1. excited　2. nervous　3. expectant

[31] **Spode:** スポード社製の陶器（高級品として有名）

[32] **damn** (= damned) などという汚い言葉遣いをしてしまった理由が under the stress of the occasion である。

[34] **All right, very well:**「いいわ、わかったわ」。言葉遣いは丁寧だが、かなり怒っている。

[36] Q. **I was only judging by the pattern** はどういう意味か？

[36] **the best part:** ほとんどの部分

[38] **a forgery** = a fake

[38] Q. **unfortunately:** なぜ、あるいは何が「不運」なのか？

[39] Q. **familiar** の意味はどれか？
1. ありふれた　2. 家族のような　3. 聞き慣れている

[39] **abrasive** [əbréisiv, -ziv]: 耳ざわりな、かんにさわる、いらいらさせられる

[40] Q. **grind within him** はどういう意味か？

[42] **following . . . in a steady career:** 同じ航跡をたどっている

[42] **the picture rail:** 額長押(がくなげし)。壁に水平に打ちつけた板。額縁などをつるすためのもの。右写真参照。

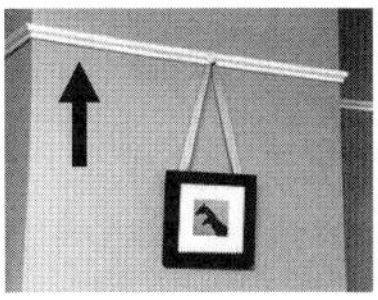

A picture rail

[44] **ha!** = nonsense!

[45] **a pair of steps:** 脚立(きゃたつ)

[48] **Obligingly** ⇐ oblige 好意を示す、願いを聞き入れる。
E.g., Kindly oblige me by closing the door. どうかドアを閉めてください。

[50] **sunny** = cheerful

[50] Q. **she was ceremonious and expert** は、Miss Pinkerton が何をしている様子の表現か？ 本文から抜き出しなさい。

'Don't touch it, don't go near it!' George pushed her aside and grabbed the steps, knocking over a blue glass bowl, a Dresden figure, a vase of flowers and a decanter of sherry; like a bull in a china shop, as Miss Pinkerton exclaimed. But she was determined, and struggled to reclaim the steps.

'Laura!' he said desperately. 'I believe it is Spode. I take your word.'

The saucer then flew out of the window.

They acted quickly. They telephoned to the local paper. A reporter would come right away. Meanwhile, Miss Pinkerton telephoned to her two scientific friends—at least, one was interested in psychic research and the other was an electrician. But she got no reply from either. George had leaned out of the window, scanning the rooftops and the night sky. He had leaned out of the back windows, had tried all the lights and the wireless. These things were as usual.

The news man arrived, accompanied by a photographer.

'There's nothing to photograph,' said Miss Pinkerton excitably. 'It went away.'

'We could take a few shots of the actual spot,' the man explained.

Miss Pinkerton looked anxiously at the result of George and the steps.

'The place is a wreck.'

Sherry from the decanter was still dripping from the sideboard. 'I'd better clear the place up. George, help me!' She fluttered nervously, and started to pack the fire with small coals.

'No, leave everything as it is,' the reporter advised her. 'Did the apparition make this mess?'

George and Miss Pinkerton spoke together.

'Well, indirectly,' said George.

'It wasn't an apparition,' said Miss Pinkerton.

The reporter settled on the nearest chair, poising his pencil and asking, 'Do you mind if I take notes?'

'Would you mind sitting over here?' said Miss Pinkerton. 'I don't use the Queen Annes normally. They are very frail pieces.'

[53] Q. **knocking over** はどういう意味か？

[53] **a Dresden:** ドレスデンチャイナ製の

[54] **a decanter:** デカンター。ワインなどを入れておく、卓上用のガラス瓶。

[54] **a bull in a china shop:**「(陶器屋で暴れる牛のように) 他人に迷惑をかけても平気な人」を表す慣用表現だが、ここはほとんど文字どおりの意味にもなっている。

[56] Q. **reclaim** はどういう意味か？

[57] Q. **take your word** はどういう意味か？

[60] Q. **the local paper** はどういう意味か？

[63] Q. **psychic research** の意味はどれか？
1. 心の探究　2. 心霊研究　3. 精神分析

[66] **the wireless** = radio

[69] **excitably** = excitedly

[73] Q. **the result of George and the steps** とは何か？

[77] Q. **clear . . . up** はどういう意味か？

[78] **the fire:** 暖炉の火

[80] Q. **apparition** はどういう意味か？

[87] **Queen Annes:** a Queen Anne の複数形。Queen Anne はイギリスのアン女王 (1665–1714) のことだが、アン女王時代 (1702–14) に流行した建築や家具の様式を指す形容詞 (「アン王朝時代の」) としても用いられる。ここでは、この様式の椅子のこと。優美な曲線の「猫足」が有名。
Cf. a Picasso 1 枚のピカソの絵。

[87] **frail** = fragile

A Dresden figure

Two Queen Anne chairs

The reporter rose as if stung, then perched on a table which Miss Pinkerton looked at uneasily.

'You see, I'm in antiques,' she rattled on, for the affair was beginning to tell on her, as George told himself. In fact he sized up that she was done for; his irritation abated, his confidence came flooding back.

'Now, Laura, sit down and take it easy.' Solicitously he pushed her into an easy chair.

'She's overwrought,' he informed the pressmen in an audible undertone.

'You say this object actually flew in this window?' suggested the reporter.

'That is correct,' said George.

The camera-man trained his apparatus on the window. 'And you were both here at the time?'

'No,' Miss Pinkerton said. 'Mr Lake was in the kitchen and I called out, of course. But he didn't see inside the bowl, only the outside, underneath where the manufacturer's mark is. I saw the pattern so I got the steps to make sure. That's how Mr Lake knocked my things over. I saw inside.'

'I am going to say something,' said George.

The men looked hopefully towards him. After a pause, George continued, 'Let us begin at the beginning.'

'Right,' said the reporter, breezing up.

'It was like this,' George said. 'I came straight in when Miss Pinkerton screamed, and there was a white convex disc, you realize, floating around up there.'

The reporter contemplated the spot indicated by George.

'It was making a hell of a racket like a cat purring,' George told him.

'Any idea what it really was?' the reporter enquired.

[88] **perched** = sat on something, especially on the edge of it.

[90] **Q. rattled on** はどういう意味か？

[91] **Q. tell on . . .** はどういう意味か？

[91] **Q. size . . . up** はどういう意味か？

[92] **done for** = exhausted

[93] **came flooding back:** 一挙に戻ってきた

[94] **Q. take it easy** はどういう意味か？

[94] **Q. Solicitously** の意味はどれか？
1. 熱心に　2. 心配して気遣うように　3. きちょうめんに

[96] **Q. audible undertone** = in a voice very (　　　) but audible to (　　　)

[101] **trained:** (カメラ、武器などを) ～に向けた (on; upon)

[101] **Q. his apparatus** = his (　　　)

[111] **breezing up** = cheering up

[112] **Q. I came straight in when Miss Pinkerton screamed** = I came in (　　　) after hearing Miss Pinkerton scream.

[113] **convex:** 凸状の。Cf. concave 凹状の。

[113] **you realize** = you see

[116] **a hell of a . . . :** ひどい～

[116] **a racket** = a loud unpleasant noise

22

Miss Pinkerton's Apocalypse

(Part 2)

Muriel Spark

George took his time to answer. 'Well, yes,' he said, 'and no.'

'Spode ware,' said Miss Pinkerton.

George continued, 'I'm not up in these things. I'm extremely sceptical as a rule. This was a new experience to me.'

'That's just it,' said Miss Pinkerton. 'Personally, I've been in china for twenty-three years. I recognized the thing immediately.'

The reporter scribbled and enquired, 'These flying discs appear frequently in China?'

'It was a saucer. I've never seen one flying before,' Miss Pinkerton explained.

'I am going to ask a question,' George said.

Miss Pinkerton continued, 'Mr Lake is an art framer. He handles old canvases but next to no antiques.'

'I am going to ask. Are you telling the story or am I?' George said.

'Perhaps Mr Lake's account first and then the lady's,' the reporter ventured.

Miss Pinkerton subsided crossly while he turned to George.

'Was the object attached to anything? No wires or anything? I mean, someone couldn't have been having a joke or something?'

George gave a decent moment to the possibility.

'No,' he then said. 'It struck me, in fact, that there was some

[3] **not up in . . .** = not knowledgeable about . . .

[5] **That's just it.** = Just the point! あるいは That's exactly the problem!

[7] Q. **These flying discs appear frequently in China?** ここにどんな誤解があるか？

[12] **art framer:** 額縁細工師

[17] Q. **venture** はどういう意味か？

[18] Q. **subside** はどういう意味か？

[22] Q. **decent** の意味はどれか？
1. それなりの　2. 立派な　3. 気品ある

An alleged flying saucer seen over Passaic, New Jersey, in 1952

sort of Mind behind it, operating from outer space. It tried to attack me, in fact.'

'Really, how was that?'

'Mr Lake was not attacked,' Miss Pinkerton stated. 'There was no danger at all. I saw the expression on the pilot's face. He was having a game with Mr Lake, grinning all over his face.'

'Pilot?' said George. 'What are you talking about—pilot!'

Miss Pinkerton sighed. 'A tiny man half the size of my finger,' she declared. 'He sat on a tiny stool. He held the little tiny steering-wheel with one hand and waved with the other. Because, there was something like a sewing-machine fixed near the rim, and he worked the tiny treadle with his foot. Mr Lake was not attacked.'

'Don't be so damn silly,' said George.

'You don't mean this?' the reporter asked her with scrutiny.

'Of course I do.'

'I would like to know something,' George demanded.

'You only saw the under side of the saucer, George.'

'You said nothing about any pilot at the time,' said George. 'I saw no pilot.'

'Mr Lake got a fright when the saucer came at him. If he hadn't been dodging he would have seen for himself.'

'You mentioned no pilot,' said George. 'Be reasonable.'

'I had no chance,' said she. She appealed to the camera-man. 'You see, I know what I'm talking about. Mr Lake thought he knew better, however. Mr Lake said, "It's a forgery." If there's one thing I do know, it's china.'

'It would be most unlikely,' said George to the reporter. 'A steering-wheel and a treadle machine these days, can you credit it?'

'The man would have fallen out,' the camera-man reflected.

'I must say,' said the reporter, 'that I favour Mr Lake's long-range theory. The lady may have been subject to some hallucination, after the shock of the saucer.'

'Quite,' said George. He whispered something to the photographer. 'Women!' Miss Pinkerton heard him breathe.

The reporter heard him also. He gave a friendly laugh. 'Shall

[24]　**Q. Mind:** なぜ大文字なのか？

[24]　**outer space:** 宇宙

[35]　**treadle** [tredl]:（ミシンなどの）ペダル

[38]　Q. **You don't mean this?** はどういう意味か？

[38]　Q. **with scrutiny** はどういう意味か？

[47]　Q. **I had no chance.** = I had no chance to（　　　）the pilot.

[55]　Q. **long-range theory** が紹介されている箇所を指摘しなさい。

[56]　**hallucination** = the fact of seeming to see or hear somebody or something that is not really there, especially because of illness or drugs

[59]　Q. **Women!** はどういう意味か？

作者のスパーク自身、仕事が忙しいときに飲んだ薬が原因で妄想を見た経験がある。スパークの伝記（Martin Stannard, *Muriel Spark: The Biography*, 2010）によれば、1954 年 1 月に食欲を抑え集中力を高める中枢神経刺激剤であるアンフェタミン製剤（デキセドリン）を服用したところ、詩人・劇作家の T・S・エリオットから脅迫のメッセージが送られてくると感じて怯えてしまったのである。エリオットの戯曲を読んでも彼女を脅す言葉ばかりだった……。

その当時エリオット（1888–1965）は存命中だったが、スパークと直接の親交はなかった。

we continue with Mr Lake's account, and then see what we can make of both stories?'

But Miss Pinkerton had come to a rapid decision. She began to display a mood hitherto unknown to George. Leaning back, she gave way to a weak and artless giggling. Her hand fluttered prettily as she spoke between gurgles of mirth. 'Oh, what a mess! What an evening! We aren't accustomed to drink, you see, and now oh dear, oh dear!'

'Are you all right, Laura?' George enquired severely.

'Yes, yes, yes,' said Miss Pinkerton, drowsy and amiable. 'We really oughtn't have done this, George. Bringing these gentlemen out. But I can't keep it up, George. Oh dear, it's been fun though.'

She was away into her giggles again. George looked bewildered. Then he looked suspicious.

'It's definitely the effect of this extraordinary phenomenon,' George said firmly to the Press.

'It was my fault, all my fault,' spluttered Miss Pinkerton.

The reporter looked at his watch. 'I can quite definitely say you saw a flying object?' he asked. 'And that you were both put out by it?'

'Put down that it was a small, round, flattish object. We both agree to that,' George said.

A spurt of delight arose from Miss Pinkerton again.

'Women, you know! It always comes down to women in the finish,' she told them. 'We had a couple of drinks.'

'Mr Lake had rather more than I did,' she added triumphantly.

'I assure you,' said George to the reporter.

'We might be fined for bringing the Press along, George. It might be an offence,' she put in.

'I assure you,' George insisted to the photographer, 'that we had a flying saucer less than an hour ago in this room.'

Miss Pinkerton giggled.

The reporter looked round the room with new eyes; and with the air of one to whom to understand all is to forgive all, he folded his notebook. The camera-man stared at the pool of

[64] **hitherto** [hìðərtúː | ⸍ ⸌] = up to now

[65] **give way to . . . :** 抑制をなくして〜に身をまかせる

[65] **artless giggling** [gíglɪŋ]**:** 自然なくすくす笑い

[68] **oh dear!:** おやまあ、あらあら

[70] **drowsy:** 眠そうな

[72] Q. **I can't keep it up** はこの文脈では具体的に何を意味しているのか？

[78] **spluttered:** まくしたてた

[81] **put out** = upset

[82] **Put down:** 書きとめなさい

[84] Q. **spurt:** ラストスパートの spurt だが、ここではどういう意味か？

[85] Q. **comes down to . . .** はどういう意味か？

[89] Q. **I assure you** は何が確かだと言っているのか？

1. 謎の小さい円盤が飛んできたこと
2. すべてが二人で組んだ狂言だったこと
3. ジョージの方がたくさん酒を飲んだこと

[91] **an offence** = criminal offence

[95] Q. **with the air of one to whom . . .** はどういう意味か？

sherry, the overturned flowers, the broken glass and china. He packed up his camera, and they went away.

George gave out the tale to his regular customers. He gave both versions, appealing to their reason to choose. Further up the road at her corner shop, Miss Pinkerton smiled tolerantly when questioned. 'Flying saucer? George is very artistic,' she would say, 'and allowances must be made for imaginative folk.' Sometimes she added that the evening had been a memorable one, 'Quite a party!'

It caused a certain amount of tittering in the neighbourhood. George felt this; but otherwise, the affair made no difference between them. Personally, I believe the story, with a preference for Miss Pinkerton's original version. She is a neighbour of mine. I have reason to believe this version because, not long afterwards, I too received a flying visitation from a saucer. The little pilot, in my case, was shy and inquisitive. He pedalled with all his might. My saucer was Royal Worcester, fake or not I can't say.

[100] **gave out:** 公表した、言いふらした

[102] **corner shop:** 街角の店

[104] **allowances must be made for . . . :** ～は大目にみてあげなければならない。意訳すれば、「想像力が豊かでいらっしゃる方のお話は、話半分にお聞きしておかなければいけませんわ」ということ。

[107] **Q. tittering:** titter とほぼ同じ意味の単語を本文から選び、ニュアンスの違いを調べなさい。

[112] **Q. received a flying visitation from a saucer** はどういう意味か？

[114] **Royal Worcester:** ロイヤルウスター。ウスター磁器。1751 年以来ウスターで製造されている高級磁器。

A Royal Worcester cup-and-saucer set

Suggested Answers to the Questions

Session 1　How to Look at Everything (Part 1)
[12] 普通の人間　[15] 3　[15] 1　[17] 学術出版物のこと　[19] 1　[24] 1　[25] 1　[36] 3　[38] 3　[40] 1　[41] 2　[42] 両手を覗き眼鏡のように目に当てる　[43] not　[46] 3　[51] 自分の才能や名声にすごいと思うようなこともすっかりなくなってしまっているということ　[55] 2　[62] 3　[66] person（character）　[66] self　[70] 自由に想像力を働かせる　[78] 2

Session 2　How to Look at Everything (Part 2)
[65] 2　[78] 79 行目の a beautiful curve から about life まで　[81] 1（この場合の particular は、ある具体的なものを指しているが、日本語の「特殊」や「特別」という語のニュアンスとは異なる）　[116] wide　[120] 3　[135] 3　[139] 1　[142] mind's eye（l. 136）

Session 3　How the Brain Creates Our Mental World (Part 1)
[5] 1　[10] only　[25] 大変な騒ぎを引き起こした　[56] 決まった関係にある、しっかりと対応する（逆は loose relationship）　[59] We とは我々の意識（consciousness）ないし認識（awareness）を指しており、脳の活動は必ずしも我々の意識・認識と一致しない　[74] for 以下のものがやってこないかと気をつけて見ている　[75] 3　[111] フレームは動かずに中の点が動いたという認識　[117] あなたをだまして～と考えさせる

Session 4　How the Brain Creates Our Mental World (Part 2)
[20] つっつく（検診のために、ああしろこうしろとうるさい）　[37] 外界に働きかけている　[41] 勝手に、ひとりでに　[42] 3　[48] 3　[48] しきりに手を伸ばして（何度も）素早く引っ張る（'To pull at something' means 'to pull something quickly and usually repeatedly'）　[51] directly　[59] tricky　[61] 3　[68] high　[69] 3　[75] not　[88] 3　[93] 自分自身に関する知識が実は不確かなものであることを明らかにしていく作業

Session 5　A Super Tunnel (Part 1)
[3] intuition（l. 5）　[7] 1　[13] 理性、直感（直観）　[21] このゲームは繰り返されることになっている　[31] must（should）　[33] change; choice（decision）　[34] opening　[53]（to）stay with your first choice（l. 46）　[63] 3　[66] 3　[68] 1　[86] 1 つの箱を開いた時点で残った 1 つが当たる確率（3 分の 2）と、最初に選んだものが当たる確率（3 分の 1）（箱を変更して当たる確率（3 分の 2）と、箱を変更しないで当たる確率（3 分の 1））　[108] 3　[113] 2

Session 6　A Super Tunnel (Part 2)

[5] 1　[6] 助かる人の名前をぎりぎりまで明かさず、死の恐怖を長く味わわせるから　[12] どんなことがあっても　[44] やりとり、取引（囚人Cが時計を与えるのと引き換えに、処刑される囚人1人の名前を教えてもらったこと）　[48] mad　[52] increase（l. 56）　[53] 1　[56] 囚人B　[57] 2　[61] weight; body（l. 62; substanceなど別解もありうる）　[74] 3　[82] 2　[86] to spare one of the condemned men（l. 5）　[94] 2　[100] ありえないこと、めちゃくちゃ

Session 7　The Pendulum Clock of Christiaan Huygens (Part 1)

[2] 3　[21] 1　[22] 3　[23] 1　[25] まず理論があって、それによって現実のものごとを説明しようとすること　[28] 2　[32] 3　[36] 2　[41] 3　[42] 2　[59] the absolute truth of the matter（l. 55）　[60] ～と照合して検証される　[61] 科学の歴史の始まり　[87] minute hand　[95] 1　[99] ガリレオが振り子の性質を発見したことがホイヘンスによる正確な時計の発明につながり、さらにこの発明がきっかけでニュートンが地球の自転の証拠を得るというように、さまざまな科学の分野が互いに意外な関連をもちながら発展すること

Session 8　The Pendulum Clock of Christiaan Huygens (Part 2)

[1] 3　[4] 船舶を使った海上での実験　[5] 1　[10] will　[11] 毎日決まった時刻に測定をする　[22] 船に積んだ飲料水が心配になるほど減ってきた　[23] 互いに食い違う計算　[26] 水を補給できるかもしれないところ　[29] 仲間（遠征隊の一行）　[33] 急いで印刷した　[35] ～が注文され出した（place an orderで「発注する」の意味）　[35] 1　[38] ホイヘンスの時計のおかげでフエゴ島に到着できたとする報告を受け入れることについて　[46] 時計を用いることによって　[65] 1　[74] 3　[80] The mostが主語で、そのあとに関係代名詞が省略され、today's Royal Society was prepared to sayが修飾語としてThe mostにかかっている　[81] all species . . . 4000 BC　[87] 1　[90] 2　[92] 急がずともよい（時が味方してくれる）　[93] 3　[97] science; other　[100] 2　[103] 格安航空券での空の旅　[104] 2

Session 9　The Secret Garden (Part 1)

[4] 2　[5] instinctive aesthetic reactions　[5] 生き残りに不利に働く、生存に悪い影響を及ぼす　[7] 2　[9] other animals　[11] 人間が動き回れること　[23] 人類が誕生したときに生息していた場所　[24] 思いがけない効果や結果　[37] 手がかり　[52] 2　[53] 3　[62] direction　[63] 1　[63] 森林におおわれた環境　[64] 生物は～に集中して生息している　[65] ground　[66] 上空をおおっている森　[72] seen　[78] 1　[86] 2　[88] could　[91] fascination（l. 83）　[93] uninterrupted（l. 102）

Session 10　The Secret Garden (Part 2)

[2] is most appreciated（we most appreciate） [9] canopies and refuges（l. 7） [13] panoramic vistas（l. 8） [16] 憩い（安全な隠れ家を提供し、ひらけた眺望もある）を与えてくれるような、人間の感性に合った建築上の工夫を無視すること [21] 情緒不安定 [50] it（to 以下のこと）をする価値がある、したほうがためになる、損にならない [57] love（fascination）, fear [61] instinctively attracted to（towards） them [64] 3 [73] 3 [79] flowers [81] flowers [91] flowers; if [94] instinct（l. 97） [98] instinct [99] 3 [110] 私たちを魅了するものの幾何学的、視覚的な模様 [112] 1 [115] 1

Session 11　Heroic Contrasts: The Extraordinary versus the Banal (Part 1)

[2] 3 [4] 協調して行う行動 [6] 協力し合うこと [10] group（team） [10] 3 [12] 3 [24] 2 [25] catalyst（触媒）は、それ自体は変わらないが他の物の変化を引き起こす物を比喩的に指す語であり、ある状況（目の前で暴漢に襲われている人がいるとか、プラットフォームから落ちそうになった人がいるとか）のせいで普通の人が英雄に変わると考えれば、その状況がその変化の触媒となったと言える [39] 1 [40] 3 [44] 2 [45] 巧みに、時に不正に組織化する、編成する [50] different [52] ordinary [55] 大量虐殺を行った者 [60] 1 [69] normal; normal [71] 1 [75] 3 [78] terrifying [86] 締めの言葉、さわりの言葉 [89] 1 [89] 3 [90] defies [94] systematic＝組織として行う、personal＝個人で行う [99] Jewish [104] 1 [114] 自分で善悪を判断する力があること、道徳的自律性 [118] 国家が認めた拷問者 [123] 田舎出身の普通の若者が、国家の武器となる

Session 12　Heroic Contrasts: The Extraordinary versus the Banal (Part 2)

[3] evil; heroism [3] 3（tendency はこの場合「傾向」ではなく「性癖」の意） [5] 3 [8] 1 [10] その場の勢い、流れ [16] 責任の拡散、すなわち集団全体の責任と感じられるために、自分個人としての責任を感じなくなること [17] 1 [19] なんらかのイデオロギーが正しいと信じて、そのために一所懸命になること [25] 3 [27]（国家などが行う）組織的な大量虐殺（ホロコーストのこと） [30] colored は黒人を指す。バスの colored section とは、バスの後方にある、黒人の乗車が許可された場所のこと [39] necessary（imperative） [40] 3 [48]（a）月桂冠（b）栄誉を称える印 [62] obeyed [64] 2 [66] 容易に状況に流される人たち [67] 1 [69] 明確な定義を受け付けない [70] 英雄的行為が行われたその場でのデータ収集 [71] heroic acts [71] 3 [74] decision matrix（決定行列）とは、さまざまな決定要因を表にして分析・比較することにより最終決定に至る表のことを指すが、ここでは比喩的に決定に至るまでの因果関係を意味している [84] 一見したところでは [85] 英雄は普通の人とは違うという myth（根拠の薄い社会通念）を否定し、英雄をたいしたものではないとみなす、矮小化するという意味 [86] 普通の人がある場面に遭遇して英雄になったり、悪人になったりするのだとする我々の考え方 [89]「役割モデル」、すなわち模範となる人物、ふるまいかたや人生のお手本 [92] a choice [93] common

Session 13　Evolved for Cancer? (Part 1)

[9] 1　[11] 裏切って私たちを攻撃する　[13] 3　[20] 自然選択（自然淘汰）は〜を選んできた　[21] wipe out　[22] 2　[30] 特殊化（分化）する、つまり、ある特定の器官や体の一部を形成する　[43] more　[44] out　[53] 厳密な意味では誰かが選択するわけではなく、進化の過程で突然変異が起こり、それがその後の子孫に継承・遺伝されていったときにそれを「選択された」と呼ぶから　[53] 2　[58] ダーウィンが提唱したような個体の変異と自然淘汰で説明される古典的な進化論　[65] 2　[67] These strategies（l. 63）　[70] 3　[71] suppress　[79] 2　[81] ハツカネズミを遺伝子操作した　[83] 1　[84] p16　[86] p16 が生み出せないように遺伝子操作をされたハツカネズミ　[87] 1　[93] 遺伝子操作をされていないハツカネズミ（rodent は齧歯類の動物）　[102] 癌を抑制する

Session 14　Evolved for Cancer? (Part 2)

[3] 困る、不安にさせられる（癌細胞がより危険なものになるから）　[4] 2　[5] ほかの猿と分かれて、人間として進化した　[7] tools　[10] 1　[13] survive（adapt）　[13] 利点のほうが、それが及ぼす害よりも大きい　[14] some [genes] that play important roles in cancer（l. 12）、または these highly evolved cancer genes（l. 14）　[22] produces（creates, makes など）　[26] 1　[36] 2　[56] 母親から栄養を摂取する胎児の能力が強くなりすぎると母親の健康が極端に悪化するし、母親の自己防衛が強くなりすぎると胎児は死んでしまうから、そこまでいかないように互いに抑えながら争っているということ　[60] 本来は胎盤を形成し、出生後は活動しない遺伝子が、癌細胞に乗っ取られること　[60] 3　[61] 通常ならば活動しないはずの時期に　[62] 腫瘍にとって役に立つ、好都合である　[64] 突然変異を繰り返して増殖していく癌細胞　[69] 〜するように突然変異した遺伝子が自然選択されて残るかもしれない　[73] 3　[78] clarify（l. 77）　[80] 薬が効かない　[83] 84 行目の chemotherapy drugs まで　[95] 急速に進化を遂げるある種の遺伝子を利用している腫瘍、すなわち癌のこと　[109] 2　[118]（生物学でいう）群体。人間の体を、遺伝子が仮に住んでいる居留地とみなしている

Session 15　Easeful Death (Part 1)

[6] 2003 年、2004 年、2005 年に提出された 3 つの安楽死法案（2–3 行目の記述参照）　[7] 2　[16] of sound mind とは「健全な精神を備えている」、すなわち「記憶力、理解力などが正常な状態にある」の意であり、of unimpaired judgement は「損なわれていない十分な判断能力がある」の意　[20] 医師自らが手を下して患者を安楽死させること　[24] 肉体的に無理（自殺したくても自分ではできないということ）　[26] 3　[26] 医師が殺人の容疑で起訴される　[28] 2　[35] すべてがそれに依拠しているような、とても重要なこと　[39] 自殺幇助　[43] 2　[44] 2　[46] 人工的な手段の介入がなく自然の摂理のままにやってくること　[46] 2　[50] 治療によって得られる効果に較べて治療費がかかりすぎる、あるいは、患者や家族にとって苦痛や負担が大きすぎるなどのこと　[58] 3　[59] 病院で死亡することが一般的になってきたということ

[69] 1　[72] should（can）　[73] 1　[77] なんらかの安楽死を合法と定めた国の立法府　[79] 同じように安楽死を合法とするということ　[80] of sound mind and unimpaired judgement（l. 16）　[81] 82 行目の be helped to die by his doctor からこの文の終わりまで　[81] そして本気でそう願っている　[81] everyone　[87] 医師が殺人罪で起訴されること　[88] 3　[95] 3　[97] ～のために最もよいと考えて　[99] 事例証拠（事例の報告にもとづく証拠）　[100] 安楽死を求めるよう患者を誘導している　[104] 3　[105] 1

Session 16　Easeful Death (Part 2)

[2] 尊厳死　[4] わずかの票差で（かろうじて過半数を得て）　[8] オレゴン州法に対する連邦政府の抑圧に歯向かおうとすること　[10] 本当に耐えがたい状態になったとき自殺することのできる薬　[12] 2　[18] 法律の条項　[22]「純粋に気高い」動機で行われた場合には自殺幇助をしても処罰されないこと　[23] several voluntary organizations　[24] 手数料を払えば、有料で　[27] 3　[30] 注意する　[32] 安楽死や自殺幇助を法律で認めたということ　[38] support［approve, accept］; oppose［disapprove, reject］　[44] 看護師（集合名詞）　[45] though（although）　[53] in response to 以下の部分と when 以下の部分を結びつけている　[59] ‘terminal illness’（what is meant by ‘terminal illness’）　[65] 1　[74] 1　[75] 尊厳死の立法化に反対する人々がよく（時に感情的になって）用いる語だが、冷静な議論では避けるべき言葉であり、本当に論理的な意味で「必然的」な因果関係がありうるかどうかについては著者として判断を保留したいため　[90] appears［takes］　[98] 人道的に安楽死が許容される場合　[101] 1　[104] 3　[109] 他者との関わり　[111] public; private（personal）　[113] 法令集に掲載される（＝法令化される）

Session 17　Great Inventions (Part 1)

[8] 2　[15]「えええっと」と、考えるような気持ち　[21] 液体が熱いなら、それを熱くしておくには熱しなければならないし、冷たいなら冷たいで冷やさなければならない。つまり、温度をそのままに保つには熱いか冷たいか分かっていなければならないはずなのに、魔法瓶は、いったいどうやって熱いのと冷たいのが分かるのだろうか、と、とぼけた問いがおもしろい　[31] 3　[33] telescope; microscope　[34] 眼鏡のレンズ　[36] 1　[44] 移住した　[47] 3　[47] 分解した　[53] view（l. 49）　[55] impossible　[59] 組み合わせる　[61] 2　[68] 何の成果にもつながらなかった　[71] 駄洒落のつもりではなく（レンズの話をしていて、フォーカスという言葉を用いたため）　[73] times　[73] 3　[84] 眼

Session 18　Great Inventions (Part 2)

[8] 中世は本当は「暗黒時代」などではないというニュアンス　[17] seem　[21] exist　[21] ～なしでは成り立たない（on 以下のものがなければ存在し得ないほど、密接に依存している）　[34] it is still less an explanation（なおさら、それは説明にならない）において否定語 still less が文頭に置かれたため、主語と動詞の倒置が起こった

[37] 1　[37] 科学の価値を信じて研究に打ちこんでいる科学者　[39] まだ存在していない、物理学の一形態（'a' は「なんらかの」というニュアンス）　[46] shaped　[48]（into 以下のものに）結実する、なる　[49] あちこちにある、分散した　[51] 共通に用いられる基本的な単位　[53] 粘土、パピルス、絵画　[63] 発明とみなされる　[66] 2　[67] 2　[70] 振り子時計を用いて正確に時刻を測れるようになったことが、ニュートン物理学など近代科学の発展をもたらした。また、自動機械としての時計のメカニズムも科学的な思考に影響を与えた（正確に動き続ける時計が自律的な自然法則の比喩として用いられるようになり、それによって科学研究がうながされたということが、66 行目の temperament に相当する）　[72] 2　[77] 2　[85] 1　[93] 2　[93] 1　[93] 知識や発想が人から人へと伝わり、シナジー（synergy）のような相乗効果を生みながら増大すること　[93] 3

Session 19　Politics, Scandal and Propaganda of Ancient Olympic Games (Part 1)

[1] 2　[1] 3　[3] 1　[3] お金がかかっていて盛大で、警備も厳重な見せ物　[4] よくよく見てみれば　[6] 政治介入。例としては、テロリストが選手を人質にする（1972 年ミュンヘンでパレスチナ解放を求める武装集団により 9 人の人質が殺された）、爆弾爆破（1996 年アトランタで、オリンピック公園に仕掛けられた爆弾で 1 人が死亡し、111 人が重軽傷を負った）、ボイコット（1980 年のモスクワオリンピックで、旧ソヴィエトのアフガニスタン侵攻に抗議して、日本を含む「西側陣営」がボイコットした）など　[10] 大いに話題になる催し　[13] localities　[15] オリンピックと名乗ってもよいと認められていた　[17] 古代ギリシャにおけるスポーツ祭典　[21] to curry favour は「勝利のために神の力添えを得るために」、in gratitude は「勝利をおさめたことを神に感謝して」　[25] 最も注目され、讃えられること　[27] cash rewards（l. 30), civic honours（l. 31）　[30] city（l. 25）　[31] 無料の食事と宿泊　[40] 2　[53] 表ざたになっていないが、シュラクサイの政治家に買収されたことが想像されるということ　[63] 3　[63] 馬車レース以外の運動競技　[76] 守護女神、この場合アテネを護る女神アテナ　[81] amphorae　[84] 1　[91] 1　[95] 3　[96] 1

Session 20　Politics, Scandal and Propaganda of Ancient Olympic Games (Part 2)

[10] 1　[11] いざこざに巻き込まれる　[16] 2　[26] 災禍をもたらした　[30] 2　[31] 2　[32] recite his poems（l. 29）　[37] took up politics（l. 35）　[41] 1　[41] 3　[49] よい宣伝になるということ　[58] 同一のレースに同じ人が何台もの馬車を出場させること　[61] enemies　[61] 2　[62] 非難　[63] 3　[64] charges against him（l. 62）　[68] 2　[77] 古代から　[78] 1　[80] 1　[81] 3　[82] オリンピア　[83] 1　[98] 1　[106] 無効な

Session 21　Miss Pinkerton's Apocalypse (Part 1)

[2] 暖炉の火を火かき棒でつっついたり、燃やしていいものを投げ込んだり、なにげないことをしている　[3] she; she　[11] 度肝を抜かれて、なかなか言葉もでないほどの動揺　[15] can't be とか、that's absolutely certain とか、強い口調で Miss Pinker-

tonの発言を否定し、彼女の気分を害した [15] tactful [16] if; for [17] because [18] I should hope . . . は、〜のことを強い感情で「そのはずだ」と思っているときに使う。『ロングマン現代英英辞典』では 'used to emphasize that you are not surprised by what someone has told you because you have moral reasons to expect it' と定義され、'He did apologise.' 'I should hope so, after the way he behaved.' という例文が挙げられている。 [19] 2 [25] 3 [26] ぎりぎりかすめて飛ぶ [29] 2 [36] 私は皿の模様だけで判断していた [38] よりによってMiss Pinkertonが（自分がプロ中のプロだと思っているが故に）むきになるような話題において彼女の鑑識眼を否定するようなことを言ったから [39] 3 [40]（彼の中できしむ⇒）彼の神経をいらだたせる [50] examine the mark（l. 46） [53] 脚立をぶつけてひっくり返す [56] 返してもらう [57] 君の言うとおりだと信じる [60] 地方新聞 [63] 2 [73] 脚立をぶつけてひっくり返す [56] 返してもらう [57] 君の言うとおりだと信じる [60] 地方新聞 [63] 2ジョージが脚立でめちゃくちゃにした室内 [77] 片付ける [80] 幽霊 [90] ぺちゃくちゃしゃべり続けた [91] こたえる、〜にとってつらくなる [91]（口語で）情勢などを判断する、〜と踏む [94] 気を楽にしろ、落ちつけ [94] 2 [96] low（quiet, small）; them [101] camera [112] immediately

Session 22 Miss Pinkerton's Apocalypse (Part 2)

[7] in china（陶器を扱ってきた、商ってきた）を「中国にいた」という意味にとった [17] Miss PinkertonとMr Lakeの様子が険悪になってきたので、あえて口をはさんでみた [18] 静まる [22] 1（頭ごなしに否定してしまったら相手に失礼なので） [24] ある一人の人間の心ではなく、人間の常識を越えた高度な知性を意味するため [38] まさか、ご冗談でしょう？ [38] 探るように、本当かどうか吟味するように [47] mention [55] that there was some sort of Mind behind it, operating from outer space（ll. 23–24） [59]「まったく女ってものは！」（女性は理性的でないとか、思い込みが激しいとかいった偏見をこめた発言） [72] 慣れない酒を飲んで思いついた悪ふざけを、もはや続けることはできない、ということ [84]（感情などの）ほとばしり、噴出 [85] 結局〜が問題だったということになる、〜に帰着する [89] 1 [95] このtoは「〜にとって」の意。「その人にとって、すべてを理解することはすべてを許すことであるというような人の雰囲気（air）をもって」⇒「今回の騒動がすべて狂言だったことを理解した上で、許してあげましょうという雰囲気を漂わせながら」 [107] giggle（l. 65）. giggleもtitterも「くすくす笑い（をする）」の意。giggleは、短く突発的な、軽い笑いといった感じ。10代の女の子の笑いが連想されることが多い。titterは、そわそわしたときなどに漏らす忍び笑い。ちなみにchuckleは、喜びや満足が連想される。 [112] 私のところにも皿が飛んできた

Index

東京大学教養英語読本 I

2013年2月20日　初　版
2023年4月10日　第9刷

［検印廃止］

編　者　東京大学教養学部英語部会

発行所　一般財団法人 東京大学出版会

代表者　吉見俊哉

153-0041 東京都目黒区駒場 4-5-29
電話：03-6407-1069・FAX：03-6407-1991
振　替　00160-6-59964

印刷所　株式会社三秀舎
製本所　牧製本印刷株式会社

ISBN 978-4-13-082132-2　Printed in Japan

切り取り線

27 ページ用切り抜き窓

四角を切りぬいて、27 ページの図の A と B にあてはめてみましょう。

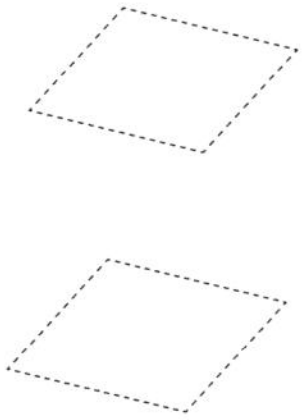